I am a "Possibilitarian! [illegible] ou will be too! I love Paulette' [illegible] e with your best friend who is telling you like it is! We all need THAT person in our lives! Her book is a roadmap for becoming who we really are and making a difference in this world doing what we love! She warns you about the potholes and detours and lays out a plan to success!

As a current client of hers, I can tell you that she is the real deal! Knowledgeable, encouraging, inspiring, empathetic, fun, and when necessary, one helluva of a good ass-kicker! If you want to unfold into your true becoming; get that business you've always wanted off the ground; and make a difference in this world, then start by reading this book!

***Victoria Downs**, Healer, Yogi*

Creatives can be abundant!

Paulette teaches her "turn your light full on, no dimmer switch" magic, inspiring creatives like me to live our best life! Paulette and her book are the real deal, and her easy way gives me confidence I can really do this: make money and be creative at the same time.

Kathy Milburn**, author of **Taking Care of the Special Needs Mom

Grab your pen and your notebook and get ready to work. Paulette is going to build your level of excitement to fever pitch and then lead you through numerous exercises designed to get you digging deep and unearthing your dreams and the blocks to your success. You will undoubtedly come back to this book again and again for attitude adjustment and motivation.You can and will be your best self. Wahoo!

***Barbara Graham**, Price, dancer*

If you've ever worked with Paulette, you know that she's infectious. Her belief in you is what makes her so incredible. How often do you tell yourself that if you only knew what you want you could change, be successful, follow the recipe you'll get it right? Years of self doubt and self sabotage built up barriers to what I really wanted for myself. She gives the tools to rewrite your story - her words echoing in my heart, head and soul now ever present as the world of creative potential awaits.

Paulette's new book is that smile, hug, voice into your potential that is there at your fingertips. If you ever feel the need to explore your limitless boundaries- start here.

***Angie Wimmer**, Master Teacher, dancer, artist, nurse*

~~~~~~

What a most fabulous, inspired read!

That inner crone wisdom she weaves into tapestries of pure beauty, with those eyes that stare deep into your soul ....encouraging you to delve deeper and explore further your own existence.

A charming almanac of how to create and live an inspired, bigger, more abundant life!

It's not just a book, but a glimpse into her soul, an anthology of heartfelt poems, it's a guide with a toolbox ripe to instigate into your own life, a workbook with challenging self-reflection exercises to ponder, a well intended self help guide to gain the clarity so you can "jump" into the life you truly desire... and deserve.

I would highly recommend this book to anyone feeling the 'stuckness" of a half lived life!

***Richelle Spencer**, Master Teacher, dancer*

~~~~~~

The heart with which Paulette writes is palpable. Her spirit of encouragement and joy leap off the page and into your being! Part cheerleader and part wise sage, Paulette not only makes me feel as though I can accomplish anything, but she's given us the practical tools for making real and lasting change in our lives and our art. "From Soulless Job to Creative Abundance" is not only a guidebook for transformation; it's a manifesto on how none of us should settle for anything less than abundance, deliciousness and joy!

***Tamie Cook**, Culinary Connector, Tamie Cook Culinary Productions*

~~~~~~

Paulette is a true champion of the creative potential within each person. She is like a cheerleader for all things possible. From her poetry to her wisdom to her life experience, she guides one through the process of living out dreams...if one does the hard work to get there. Altho her message is primarily written in language directed at women, it can be appropriated as truth for men. Paulette, with her wild, free, colorful spirit has lifted me from a constrained place to new creative expressions. Let her be a champion of your unfulfilled dreams. You won't regret it.

JeanAnne Swope

~~~~~~

FROM SOULLESS JOB TO CREATIVE ABUNDANCE

FROM SOULLESS JOB TO CREATIVE ABUNDANCE
by Paulette Rees-Denis

Published by Cultivator Press, Palm Springs, CA, 2020

DISCLAIMER

Neither the author nor the publisher assumes any responsibility for errors, omissions, or contrary interpretations of the subject matter herein. Any perceived slight of any individual or organization is purely unintentional.

Brand and product names are trademarks or registered trademarks of their respective owners.

From Soulless Job to Creative Abundance

FIND FULFILLMENT AND PROSPERITY WITH YOUR ART

by

Paulette Rees-Denis

Cultivator Press

TABLE OF CONTENTS

CHAPTER 1

WHAT ALL IS POSSIBLE?

"And the day came when the risk to remain tight in a bud was more painful than the risk it took to blossom."

~ ***Anais Nin*** ~

WELCOME TO MY DELICIOUS world of change and possibilities! This is the beautiful place where you are guided to dance with your desires, leap big into your dreams, bring your creativity to the forefront, and step up into the joyful and satisfying career you've been waiting to start. Make a change. Blossom into all your possibilities.

To be a possibilitarian!

Don't you love that word? Possibilitarian: to open up to all you are, can do, and can become. The world is waiting for you. Your people are waiting for you. Your creative spirit is waiting to be unleashed.

What all is possible?

Now is your time, my friend, because you are tired of the job you've been slogging away at. You feel like your soul has been sucked out of you. You have had it; you're fed up with not being rewarded for your hard work. You are not seen for what you have to offer. You know deep down deep in that amazingly creative heart, body, and soul that you are here to do more, to make an impact with your art, your dance, your words.

You are ready to stand up and home in on your creative genius. Really, you just want to live every day with a deeper purpose, more freedom and lightness, and even more financial prosperity. Isn't it time? Isn't it time for you to share what has been aching in you to come out? Haven't you been doing this crappy job long enough with not enough satisfaction, money, and love?

Have you seen the comedy movie *9 to 5,* with Dolly Parton, Jane Fonda, and Lily Tomlin, from 1980? Besides the fact that Dolly Parton is one of my all-time heroes, the theme song that she wrote is a worker's national anthem for sure, plus the movie is hilarious.. She sings about stumbling out of bed every day and not being excited going to work and working for someone who doesn't appreciate her at all... pretty much a hellish situation. Have you ever felt like this when you start your workday?

Here's the video link if you want to sing along! *https://www.youtube.com/watch?v=UbxUSsFXYo4*

Maybe your job is not really a crappy job but it is not how you want to spend your days, your time. It's not what you dreamed of many years ago when you had more of an idealistic idea of what you wanted to do, the change you could make in the world, living that lifestyle full of freedom and travel and abundance. But somehow, that died as you started adulting. Your dreams got pushed back. Maybe you got the partner, the kids, the house, the car, the job, but it's not how you expected your life to turn out.

Or perhaps that was what you wanted then, but now it's time to add another dimension, time for a change for you! Your creative juju is dying to come out. I do mean that it is dying, dying inside you, because you are not tapped in and turned on to it. You aren't keeping it alive. It is squashed, hidden, blocked. It's in the closet waiting for you to open the door and shed some light on it. And you aren't sure what steps to take next so you wait.

On the Verge of Becoming

I have seen so many women *on the verge of becoming*, standing up, sharing their amazingness, and yet they back down for so many reasons. "It's easy to stay small," they say. They have a certain level of comfort and don't want to leave that zone. They don't feel like their vision is important or that what they have to say, to contribute, is worthy. There is too much competition and others are better than them. It has been done before. No one wants to read their poetry or they won't be able to find students for the class they want to teach or they are not good enough. They suffer from imposter syndrome, thinking they don't know enough. They feel inadequate with lots of self-doubt.

Does any of that sound like you?

Well friend, I'm here to tell you a thing or two! *You* are so worth it, my love. Your words need to be read or heard. Your dance needs to be taught and seen. Your paintings need to grace other walls. Your lessons need to be taught and shared. Your designs are wanting to be someone's website. Someone out there is waiting for you. The universe is waiting for you to say, "Hell yeah, this is my time and look what I have to offer!"

You, dear one, is all you've got. Not your house or your friends or your car or your cabin in the woods, although all those things are pluses and part of your dreams and desires. But you, everything inside that brain, that body, heart, soul, is what you have to give, share, give back, teach, and make a difference. What you have will touch one person who then touches another and then another, that lovely trickle-down effect! Pass it on. This is living, and making a difference in the world. To create a world you want to live in is what is next for you.

"Be the change you want to see in the world."

– Mahatma Gandhi

All those creative feelings and ideas inside you are wanting to explode. Other people are wanting what you have to give – your inspiration, stories, acquired skills, beautiful vision of art and beauty and creation and life. So they too can experience a different vision of life, art, beauty, creation, so they know that they can step up into their vision too.

I don't know about you but I want to be wowed! I want to see people in their glory and light up the sky. I want to be uplifted by each person's unique individual vision and creative spirit. I want to see people shine. I want to read words that make me gasp. I want to see a dance performance where someone pours out their heart with their body. I want to see someone dress with an eye for color and delight. I want to see a flock of birds soar in that incredible V shape. I want to see chunky jewelry that someone put together with magic and intention. I want to watch a bud burst open. These things turn me on and inspire me too. That's what I do as your coach. You can call me an up-lifter, a teacher, hostess, or an inspirator. My role here is to be your guide, movement motivator, magic maker, and passion instigator.

Back thirty-ish years ago, when I first moved to Portland, Oregon, from San Francisco, California, I was creating another new chapter in my life story! With a plethora of art-filled skills and healing modalities in my pocket, I continued to build my dream of being a wild-and-free creative. I was an obsessed sacred rebel. There were, and are, many labels attached to my interests: being a tattooed underground belly-dancing rock musician, photographer, writer, tarot reader, healer, massage therapist, and budding entrepreneur, among a few other things! Seriously, I loved everything I was doing and sharing and teaching, and even working a mundane job (in my eyes at that time) as a professional photographers' printer.

I wasn't sure how to tie all these seemingly-unrelated skills together. My father used to say to me,

"When will you settle down and do one thing?" And I would say, "Never; there are too many things I want to do in life. There is too much to experience!" So, I trusted in my desires, my visions, and what the world had to offer and forged my path forward without outside help. Sure, I saw a therapist now and then, but this was before business and life coaches were popular, before computers, and so I just wrote my own book. I was starting to read books on how to succeed in the world of my weirdness from my favorites (think Starhawk, Black Elk, Shakti Gawain, and now more into the current favorites, Abraham, Tony Robbins, Wayne Dyer, Jen Sincero, Napoleon Hill), so I knew that I was not alone, that I could live my creative dreams, somehow, and make a change.

I also believed in giving back, so even if I had a few too many jobs as a DLOS (does lots of stuff), I wanted to offer a bit of myself as a way to give back to my community, to volunteer my time. With a big interest in helping youth, I volunteered at a children's homeless shelter. Working with some of them, I realized that they too had a creative soul but were lost. I wanted to help them and show these unfortunate, young homeless kids that they could find their way in the world and that it was okay, even fantastic, to be their weird self. They could fly their freak flag, they could be tattooed and still run a successful business. There was a place for them in the world. I wanted them to know that they could use their creativity to their advantage, that they could move out of unfortunate circumstances and create the life they were wanting and move forward into a prosperous and exciting life.

I wanted to show them that if I could do it, they could too. If I could help just one kid know that they had a chance and that they could bring their inner vision into reality, then my time was well spent.

This was when I figured out part of my true calling was not just to create art, but to lead others, to show that there is a place for everyone in the world! I love bringing people together as a hostess of sorts, to share and teach and uplift. As a teacher and a coach, I have been living this dream ever since.

Back to you. You've been wanting something different too and I'm here to show you how to shine your light, live the life you've been dreaming of, and move out of your unfortunate circumstances to the abundant creative life you are ready to step into. You deserve to feel good in your body, heart, and soul, and do the work you love to do – really, this is about your whole life!

Are you ready to take the time now, to first take a step back to get that overview of your life as you are living it? Are you ready to take the steps forward into the *you* that you are wanting to become? It's time to bring you more prosperity, happiness, fulfillment, satisfaction, and to feel great.

Ultimately, we are here to feel good and live to the fullest! It is our right and purpose on this planet. However, the choice is yours. Only you can make the choice to be happy, to make the changes, to create your life as you want it. You are the creator of your life. You decide and you move into what you are wanting. You create your opportunities – do you want to stay in this soul-sucking job or situation or move into more rewarding, life-enhancing possibilities? Where do you want to be a year from now?

That is what I want for you – I want to see you shine your light. Live lit up every day, be illuminated… create what your heart and soul and body want you to express and share.

I so believe we are all creative individuals on so many levels. Where does your creative zone of genius lie? Are you dreaming of cooking a fine, delicious meal for your family or a room full of folks? How about creating a painted body of work that shifts people's perspectives? Maybe you're writing poetry that makes someone's heart sing or someone else shed tears of remembrance. Perhaps you help someone else shine their light and that is your finest reward.

Tribe

We all want connection, to be a part of something. I will repeat this over and over. We humans are not solo-life dwellers. We create, share, give, and take. We also touch and listen and talk and love. We have a longing to be connected, even when we create on our own.

Think of all of us as one giant connected circle: a large family. A tribe.

What is a tribe? A tribe is a group of people or a community with similar values or interests. Sometimes, it is related by ethnicity, sometimes by blood relations, often today by interests and hobbies. But the point is the coming together with connection.

There is no beginning or ending to the circle as it continues to spiral around and around. Everyone in that circle is important to the family, the tribe. Everyone has a contribution to make the circle stronger and more enjoyable. A task, a shared experience, a helping hand, a creative vision… each individual has a role, a gift, to share and inspire, make the tribe brighter, shed some light, and support each other.

We all have so much to offer and some of us often take what we have for granted. Or we don't pay attention to what is going on inside us and push things away, brushing off our roles. As if we aren't important, or worth it… within or without the tribe, you are here to find and shine your light. Live your life as you desire. Then you find your tribe that lifts you up and that you also uplift.

Your Opportunities

First, you create your own opportunities. Those can continue to be within your soul-sucking job that won't get you anywhere. Are you willing to stay there? To be safe? Or are you ready to create the change you wish to be? To live and love full-on, to share your heart and soul, and find the satisfaction and the financial rewards of choosing you?

Life is for living and for loving. Love what you do. Love, people, that's what I'm talking about. To live everyday with magic and love, with sprinkles of joy and creative brilliance. No stress, no backtalk, no tears. Only with the delight of your journey as it continues to blossom and unfold.

Are you ready to find your voice and vision?

As Marianne Williamson said, "Our deepest fear is not that we are inadequate. Our deepest fear is that we are powerful beyond measure. It is our light, not our darkness, that most frightens us. We ask ourselves, who am I to be brilliant, gorgeous, talented, fabulous? Actually, who are you not to be?"

You see, my friend, that light within you is waiting to be turned on, and full on, no dimmer switch here! Allow your voice to awaken and rise, to release, and be heard. I leave you with a poem of mine; I call these my life shorts. I hope you can feel my heart and soul as I share this, and more of these throughout the book, as I too, have opened up to my creative abundance, here through the power of the word. I can't wait to see you in the next chapter.

MY VOICE

Paulette Rees-Denis

The water is flowing
Through my body
As the hips circle the unknown
Mama Bear is coming
As the trickle of the creek turns
Into a gushing waterway
Unlocking the mysteries
The hibernating queen strolls
Into the open
Opening her heart to me
Not in the gnawing-gashing-bloody-rip-my-
heart-out kind of way
But in the gentle-waking-up-opening-my-eyes-to-
the-new-world
kind of way
I am untethered now, my freedom soars
as the river pulses, over the rocks
I flow with it
shredding pieces of my flesh, of quiet, of walls of
holding back, of release
my voice is coming, at first, softly, but not timid,
gathering the momentum of the river, from the
belly of mama bear,
To awake and rise, to release, and be heard
It slithers like a snake, finding its way,
Over the river and through the woods
Walking with the mother, she takes my hand
And allows me to lead.

CHAPTER 2

STARTING AGAIN

Starting again,
Continuously, curiously, ceremoniously
Starting over
The morning brings newness, freshness
The ability to be, to become
The truest brightest self
Compassionate, patient, brilliant, prosperous,
The vision, the embodiment,
Of pure desire
Of deep creation
Of passionate longing
That curiosity that ebbs and flows
Like the blood red full moon
That openly dances amongst the clouds
Teasing me with her magical shine
With glimpses and glimmers of what could be
But always there, even in the darkness
Waiting
For the expansion

~ **Paulette Rees-Denis** ~

WHAT IS YOUR DEEP desire? What is it you are feeling? Or not feeling? Have you had the gut ache for something different but you can't even put a name on it? Have you ever said, "I know there is something different waiting for me, but I don't know what it is. I don't want to do this job forever. It's not my calling. I can feel it in my belly"?

We are going to find out, my friend. So, what is desire? Desire is a longing for something that will bring you satisfaction. It can be a craving for or an aching feeling of wanting, a thirst for, a yearning. Do you feel that when you say those words? What are you feeling passionate about? Having intense emotions for? What are you aching to create?

To Dance with Your Desires

You are desiring to be taken on a beautiful exploratory journey to find that "thing" that you are desiring, the way to change your career and fulfill your passion.

You want to feel the rush of freedom in your movement and your body, moving solo across the studio floor, having a wild moment of ecstatic dancing in your living room, or joining in tandem with another. Perhaps you want to circle up with your tribe and experience collaboration and the co-creation of art in the moment. Bask in the delight in the flow of expression through and from your body, to the page, the canvas, the instrument.

You are craving to be on fire with yourself. To make you happen. To be the change. To live lit up every day. Shimmering with your glow. Sparking and sparkling with undying passion for life in all its glory. Illuminated, baby. That's what I'm talking about.

Wayne Dyer says, "Change the way you look at things, and the things you look at change." So, let's change it all up for you. I want you to feel the beauty and connection of your body with your words.

Thoughts become words become things.

As you define and describe more of what you want, you will find the words that resonate with your desires, and embody all that you are in every inch, pore, muscle of your body and soul. I want you to feel the ache of desire as we move from the inner you to the outer you and acknowledge your creative zone of genius and how to make it all come into fruition, into manifestation, and be all the changes. You can't not create. Just like I can't not dance.

Why do I blend the ideas of dance and desire, of dancing with your deisres? It's about embodying all that you are and all that you feel. Move forward with your heartfelt intentions. Dance through your life with grace, ease, clarity, freedom, confidence, beauty, and purpose. It's about presence and being fully present in this moment in your life.

So often in my work and my adventures, I find that women live big in their heads, heads filled with little girl dreams, unfulfilled, or adult "wants," continuously circling through their brains. And that is where those dreams and goals stay, in their heads.

There are a few *huge* factors like fear, time, and money, to name a couple. Heard of those? Those can be broken down further into many underlying reasons.

Fear: some are afraid of the unknown: fear of change, fear of failure, and even fear of success.

Time: claiming there is lack of time: "I can't find the time," or "I won't make time."

Money: much the same as above, there is not enough money: "I don't have any, I can't afford it"

Blah, blah, blah… same stories, perhaps retold, replayed, boring crap, right?

Does this sound like anything you've said to yourself when you feel ready to step into a change?

So what is it you've been wanting? Desiring?

Dreaming of? What's playing games in your head?

Dance has been almost my whole life. It is the epitome of my creative expression, movement, form, sweat, stretch, rhythm, music, beauty, ugly, and beauty. From around the age of seven through many rotations around the sun and now at age sixty-two, I can't stop dancing. I don't want to ever. It's my lifeline to all my experiences. Moving the body is so primal and comes with connection and, often, community. Plus, I feel great in my body and in-charge, knowing what it can and can't do. Self-expression is art in motion.

I've always been a creative, constantly making music, singing, writing, dancing, painting, collaging, taking photos, and adorning myself. So visual and energetic! It is spirit-fueling; dancing is like a moving meditation. Being fully present in one's body is delicious and invigorating and healing. And just freakin' fun as I embody all that life offers to me!

Through my work, I have found that dancing and just plain feel-good movement is often difficult for many women, particularly older women. Men too, find it hard to move with freedom and abandon.

Our bodies are our physical connection to our daily existence and our creativity. Times have changed quickly with the onslaught of technology. With computers and televisions, we sit way more and for longer than ever.

Taking care of this temple is what I'm talking about. What we feed it, what we put on it, and how we move it or don't move it, as the case may be. This is about committing to ourselves, to our health and wellness, practicing daily self-love and self-care to it's fullest and finest, so that we can enjoy our body, this temple of love we inhabit in our time here on earth, this one present lifetime. I'll go more into some enriching practices of self-care in a later chapter, because everything you do starts with you, and how you feel, and how your maintain your health, connection, and wellness. So you can do all that you desire.

As James Brown sings, "Get up offa that thing, dance and you'll feel better." But seriously, friend, you don't have to know how to "dance" to move that thing. Dance can encompass so many forms and styles and meanings of moving the body. And this is about dancing with your desires.

Dancing is what got me started down this amazing road of inquiry and self-reflection thirty years ago. I began to teach my newly developed style of tribal bellydance and movement; this dance style I created in the early 1990's in Portland, Oregon. My style is now known as Global Caravan or Gypsy Caravan Tribal Bellydance®. Yes, trademarked and all! I have been blessed to travel and teach this exquisite form of Divine Feminine movement with women around the globe, connecting tribes.

It also became a spiritual and healing quest for me with years of study and intuitive guidance, after witnessing dramatic and subtle shifts in awareness, connection, and passion.

With a background in classical ballet, jazz, and modern, this form of bellydance was what called to my soul. At first, I just wanted to keep dancing this style that I studied with my teacher and with the other women in class. There was something powerful that was resonating with me and busting out of my heart and soul, although I did not know what it was back then or how to understand it. I knew that I wanted it more in my life, this was super important, and that this was a calling for me, my purpose. Before I moved away from the Bay Area where I had been studying and performing with my teacher for five years, I wrapped myself up in her style that she was creating with a few of us women who would all become world dancers and leaders (that's another story!)

When I moved to Portland, I wanted a style of my own. I take great pride in artistry and integrity, as well as having the vision that I wanted to bring women of the world together. Now, mind you, this was before computers and the internet and over the years, I developed this signature style of dance: Global Caravan/Gypsy Caravan Tribal Bellydance.

What happened as my dance classes grew was profound within me but also within my students. Whoa… I had to figure this out. What was happening when these women danced together? When they moved their bodies in sensual, feminine, delicious curvy movements? Changes, friends, changes on so many levels…

My students started falling in love with themselves again or for the first time! My dance classes became part of a new community, connection, a circle of beauty and power. That connection as part of human needs. Looking at themselves in the mirrors. Performing. Laughing, Lots of tears. Okay, this was powerful stuff… but what was going on?

I dove deeper into myself and into the history of dance, spiritual movement, magical desires, ancient healing rites, mythology, and old stories. I also really wanted to look at the relevance of how this was fitting into modern society from a dance that had quite a history. My dance styling was new and contemporary and what I found out was that everyone woman who saw it, saw me, saw us, wanted what we were having!

I have already written my part-experiential book, part-memoir entitled *Tribal Vision: The Celebration of Life Through Tribal Belly Dance*, published by my own publishing company, Cultivator Press, in 2008. You can read that book to get more of this past juice and development. I want to bring you forward into my current work with a more intense and curious focus, having a passionate embrace with life and creativity, with a whole connection of body, heart, mind, and soul.

To fully envelope life and your creative zone and live full-on takes being connected on all levels – spiritually, physically, and emotionally. Those are the components of my work and our journey together.

I went from studying to creating, bringing all aspects of life into the dance, and becoming a globally-sought-after teacher. What and how I was teaching was having a major impact on my students. I was diving in and bringing in different components of healing and creating and beauty into the dance classes; I was including experiential-type exercises, not only in the dance itself, but also with connections to each other, moving meditations, and co-creating. This was powerful stuff and it was blowing my mind.

I was seeing profound effects on my students. These women (and a few men!) were finding more happiness within themselves. Besides working and strengthening their bodies, this was such a feminine dance that they were feeling their juiciness, their own beauty in the power of their hips and bellies and shoulders. All parts, all connected. They were looking at themselves in the mirror and loving their bodies and their age. One class a week, or four, they were changing their energy, and feeling happier, adorning their bodies with color and jewelry from the dance styling and mixing of cultures. They were taking more time for self-care, getting massages and pedicures, and taking time for themselves. It was fun, physically challenging, and emotionally rewarding; it was creating and had a spiritual connection.

We all want to be seen and heard. We are here to take up space, and that was an important aspect of what I was teaching, to not fall back into a corner or be quiet or submissive. We are born to be creative creatures. These gorgeous women were starting to add even more creative power to their lives, which also became their side-hustle or new career. Doors were opening to new adventures. Some got pregnant; some left their relationships. Others fell in love. Some started sewing costumes, some started making jewelry and body ornaments, some started writing poetry. Others were painting. All the things could happen. And this too was a new way to make money, to share their passions and create an income, and a life of their dreams.

So you see, the market is wide-open for all kinds of creativity. People want what you do as long as they know why you do it! You are inspired, have a vision, and want to bring more happiness and beauty and art to the world!

Because they were feeling good about themselves, this mindset shift brought more happiness and connection into the jobs some of them already had. Shifting the way you look at things and what you add to your life can make such an impact on attitude. They were taking time to hang out with the others and have more fun! Imagine what laughter does to your whole system! Spend time with things that ring your chimes. Fun, my friend, is essential to living a vibrant, full, and creative life. This is self-care at its finest! Taking time to find out what is fun for you, doing those delightful things, not shoving them into the back corner for a rainy day… oh, yes, I've done that too. As I have continued, I know that adding more fun and adventures into my daily life helps fuel my own creative path.

From teacher to leader and transformational lifestyle and business coach, I am continuously studying and building my toolbox. My growth is essential to living, as is yours! I have continued to facilitate amazing life-changing retreats and workshops around the globe. I now teach the teachers and have developed Teacher Training programs as well as virtual retreats, masterminds, and online learning for people who wanted to make small or big changes and build their careers too. I know that I can help create change by empowering others to honor themselves and listen to their heart and soul.

Here's a story of one of my current clients:

Dina has completely inspired me! Several months ago, she came to me, feeling super overwhelmed and stuck in her dead-end job. It was especially challenging because she felt like she could never make more money and she wasn't living her soul's dream of being a successful artist, or even finding time to make her art. It was impacting the rest of her life as well. I know she was frustrated and she wasn't sure of what steps to take to make some dramatic changes, even feeling unworthy to try. While a part of her was hopeful, another part of her felt like she was going to be stuck with this forever.

After three months of working with me, she had a major shift. Seeing where she could go and all her possibilities, she was already making big changes and had many new tools to make her dream work come into fruition! She attributes this shift to working with me weekly to change her state and rewrite her story.

And now, Dina's life is quite strikingly different. Wow, she committed to herself to go forward full-on to make those changes, not letting anyone or anything hold her back. Beginning with a commitment to herself, deep inner connection, getting intense clarity and feeling that desire to shift and expand into her creative zone of genius, she then quit her job and started her new career as a full-time creative.

I am so grateful to do this work and make a difference. Helping people shift from having a soul-sucking job and a feeling of overwhelm to a career of satisfaction and immense creativity with prosperity gives me more fulfillment than you could possibly know. I love seeing my clients step into their bodies, power, and creative zone of genius.

My passion is to help you to see your possibilities and all that you can create and lay the groundwork and the intricacies of opening yourself up to all that you are. All that you can become, to become a possibilitarian and step into your genius and purpose!

Movement, momentum, and magic! With the exercises in this book, you can start creating change. You will be listening to what your body needs and then feeding it what it asks for. I'm going to guide you to that place of inner and outer connection with your creative zone of genius! You will see how to build your momentum. This leads to creating everyday magic for your life.

Movement, in any form, whether that be in your body, mind, or soul, is vital for your health and wellness and vibrancy and energy. Oh, yes. What is it asking for? Does it want to shake? Do it. Dance? Do it. Stretch? Do it! Move it... you have to keep your joints juiced up, especially as we get older. Get your momentum going. Have the itch to write more poetry? Listen to it and do it! Share your gift of jewelry making? Have a dinner party for twenty in your own pop-up restaurant? You have got to love and enjoy being in your temple of love.

You have to want to take more time to listen in. What are you wanting to create?

It's called a decision. Only you have the choice. You want to decide that you are ready to take the leap or the small step or dive out of the freakin' airplane. All good! When you do, that's it; every other thing is cut off. There's only one way: your new story, your new desire. Dance some more with it and enjoy it!

A new you with a new story, living the life of your dreams, starts with you. Self-love to the highest extent. Divine self-care. You are all you have. You are here to experience and enjoy life and feel freakin' great in your skin. You want to have that deep connection with yourself in every way: body, mind, and spirit.

Whether that magic appears in the awakening connecting you have found to your body, an opening of your heart, a deeper dive into life, or just the fostering of an appreciation for life as a dance, all of us are touched by this magic of movement.

I always get so excited and curious to read about your experiences… the changes and revelations you have as you come into your bodies, souls, to dance, no matter what style or way you choose to dance and walk through life!

Six Basic Human Needs

In my coaching certification studies with my mentor and his company, Tony Robbins, he always talked about the six basic human needs: connection and love, variety and uncertainty, certainty and comfort, significance, growth, and contribution.

Think about this and where you fall into the needs and desires. What do you have a stronger calling toward?

The idea is to balance out all of these, although some are stronger or weaker than others, to help guide you to live your life as you desire and to meet your needs so you too can meet others' with your work.

One of these is the need for connection. We humans all have a desire for connection, first with self, with our body, with our heart and soul and brain. Then we all want connection with others. We want to be seen and heard, to be part of something bigger. And we want to love and be loved.

Think about variety. You, as a creative artist, want to create something different, something new, inspired. To allow the flow of creation, from within, is awesome in and of itself. Being uncertain and being present can be magic. Just wowza, having that moment of your flow, pouring out of you. Maybe you haven't felt that in a long time, having no time or space or whatever you are lacking, to create.

Then there is certainty, because we all want to be comfortable and not stress about where we might live or whether our income is enough to pay the bills. Sometimes, we fall in the too-comfortable side of things and decide to stay there because it is easy. You ever been there?

We want to feel significant, wanted, needed, loved, seen, heard. You as a creative have something to share, to enlighten another, perhaps, so that you too are seen. To feel important and a part of a bigger whole. I see you and you are here.

How can we not continue to grow, as creatives, as individuals, artists? Self-education is the way these days, which is awesome with the plethora of teachers and leaders and courses. We are meant to continually expand, learn, build upon our dreams, live in this ever expanding world, and make a difference.

This leads us to the last human need of contribution. We must continue to remain a part of this life, be connected, grow within our work and our life, and give back. There are so many ways to give back, donate, volunteer, be of service, share, and inspire. Who wants to live a life of abundance if there is not full circle to the joy of giving and receiving, of raising awareness, of standing up for what you believe in? To live deep within your values is so satisfying.

I am quite an animal rights advocate, speaking up for those who don't have a voice. That is part of my mission in my life, as a vegan, an animal lover, to share my passion of supporting the causes that ring true to my heart. So, as I am able to live a life of fulfillment, I continue to spread information, news, or opportunities to get others involved. I also belong to a women's organization that raises money to help high school students carry on and that is so cool. Giving back, my friend, fills me with deep gratitude for the life I live and how I can continue to grow and evolve. And you can do that too and see how it feeds your soul, your art, your life.

Combining discovery and creation, with movement and connection, and understanding more about human needs has brought so much more depth into my work as a coach, a writer, and a teacher. It is about creating magic and being present in our bodies, our thoughts, and our true desires. Now, this is your time to show up, to shake things up, and claim all that you are.

CHAPTER 3

THE MAKEOVER

You know that feeling of being
In overwhelm not seeing clearly
The vision you once had
Feeling stuck
Feel like you have settled for mediocrity
Of wanting more
Desiring to step up in your life
Of wanting to feel great, better
In your own skin
Of owning your dreams
Because you are tired of ignoring that ache inside
Tired of putting your dreams last
What if I can help you find liberation
And support all areas of life,
Saying YES
It's the female awakening
The makeover as you unfold into your desires
Listen to that ache and
Live that inspired life

Find clarity in your visions
For a fulfilling and empowering life
More rewarding
To get out of the rut
The box
To find freedom in movement
To soar with your passions

~ **Paulette Rees-Denis** ~

YOU ARE HERE TO shine and to live lit up every day. You want to live with that creative enthusiasm and passion. Am I right?

When I get to share my work with someone who is questioning their purpose, who is questing after their dream and ready to make a change, this just makes my spirit soar with so much love. It is a dream for me to have a client that is asking for guidance to make that change into their creative desires. My heart swells when someone stands up and says, "I am ready and willing to do the work to make a difference in my life, as well as others. And not just at twenty percent, but at 100 percent." Then we both experience a *Hell Yeah, let's do this thing together!*

What happens along the way as we do this work together? I know you are curious about the work that goes into rewriting your life and where and how you get started. To begin, I'll share some highlights of your next few steps and where we go from here.

In Chapter Four, we are going to get curious and play with ideas. Know that we all have a special purpose here on this planet, a unique gift, and sometimes we get lost on the path. It really is all part of your journey. To discover how to get back on your path, the one that is calling out to you, we will create that new way of working as we dive into all aspects of you – physical, mental, and spiritual. Think of this as your full body-and-soul makeover! Sounds fun, yes?

Imagine feeling looser and juicier in your body and creative spirit! How about the idea of waking up with the excitement to get up every day and go to work. In Chapter Five, I will be showing you an invigorating daily routine with a combo of feel-good practices, like journaling, meditation, gratitude (that's *huge!*) and a few movement ideas to get you and your joints juiced up! This will set you up and set up your day, work, fun, and projects for success. Soon you will be dancing with your desires and embodying all that you are and dream of. Hot damn!

And while we are at it, let's redefine your sexy and reawaken your feminine spirit. Don't you want to feel alive and juicy and beautiful in that body? What does it feel like to be you? Connecting with our power center, our belly, our womb is where we birth our ideas. When you can walk tall and own that body, moving forward with creative intention and confidence, in alignment with all that you are, the world is yours. And to love being in your skin is juicy and delicious. Allowing pleasure to seep through your pores and into your artwork happens because of your new connections with your inner being, with your body, and with spirit.

After we change your state, it's the exciting time of rewriting your story, which we will start in Chapter

Six. It will be time to change your words, your story, which always leads to changing your life! We'll work on releasing those old stories you've been telling yourself, the past bits you've hung on to thinking they were always going to be a part of your life. I used to feel that I had a brick wall around my heart. I realized that I was the only one who built it and it wasn't doing me any good or allowing me to move forward with my life. I had to be the one to make a change. So, little by little, I broke that wall down to allow myself to feel and reach out and create that change for myself. You can do it too. Let's knock down the walls that have imprisoned you and held you back. You don't want them anymore and this will open you up to all the new stories.

You will learn to rewrite your job, art, and life the way you truly want it to be. Oh, and we will dive into your money story too, in Chapter Seven, and change that up. I bet you already are starting to feel the letting go, the weight lifting off your shoulders, and opening up to your possibilities just by reading this book so far. I will show you how to move forward with delicious intention, right from your heart.

As a creative and soon-to-be entrepreneur of your creative self, what are your superpowers? Know your strengths, creative visions, and acknowledge all that you are. What makes you, you? This is super important as you identify all that you are and stand up to show up!

Not only do I share some woo with you (meaning I get into more spiritual and deep inner work), but I also help you lay the groundwork with practical and actionable steps. You have to do all the work and take the steps. In Chapter Eight we combine all of that in your Magic Action Plan, which is your map to success and fulfillment. I believe in creating everyday magic in all that we do, feeling good on the inside as well as the outside, and getting shit done. So, let's map out your creative adventures and have a great time doing it.

There is an art to showing up, and we'll talk about that in Chapter Nine. You are going to show up with passion and enthusiasm, living your unique calling, your deeper desires, and make those changes you've had swirling around in your head for some time now. You were not meant to stay small, you were born to stand out, to show up, to take up space!

Also, learning to live with abundance and prosperity. Gaining clarity on what you really want is delicious and necessary, so we'll learn how to ask for what you want and then let it unfold.

I want to show you how to draw what you want to you, to become a magnet. We'll go over some methods using the Law of Attraction. I'll tell you how to open up to the art of allowing and receiving. We're going downriver, my friend, with ease, flow, and continuous creativity.

You will be able to stand in your creative zone of genius, feel your glory, your authentic self, and really see how all of your desires can unfold for you with confidence and clarity. Knowing why you want to create your work, who it's for, and your true purpose will feel so good.

With new daily practices, always incorporating your gratitude habit into your daily life, you move forward with celebration! Yes, always acknowledging and celebrating all your moves, wins, and changes. From baby steps to big leaps, you are moving forward, building momentum and creating your new path and creative adventure. We learn how to always be present and notice how it is to be in the moment and enjoy the journey. Remember, it is not always the end product, but the path to get there that is full of magic and beauty, connection and creativity.

The thing about working with me is I can be a badass coach; I can kick butt but I will also hold your hand and lift you up. I want to help hold you accountable to take the actions that will help you grow into those dreams. You will have to do this work. I love the journey and I want to make it fun for you too so you can live your purpose, feel the beauty of fulfillment and prosperity, and make the world a better place to be. You are so worth it.

CHAPTER 4

GETTING CLARITY ON YOUR TRUE DESIRES

I saw the open land behind the closed fence
And I want to find the key to unlatch the lock
And sense all there is to know…
Opening up the floodgates…

~ ***Paulette Rees-Denis*** ~

SO, MY FRIEND, I want to know what you are truly wanting and desiring. What are you hungry for, to change, or to add to your life right now? What are you aching to make, feeling that creation deep down in your bones, your belly, your heart, your womb? Something new is calling you. That is very exciting!

I will ask you lots of questions and I want to give you exercises to do mentally and physically to get you grooving and moving forward!

I want to know what your creative zone of genius is. It's that thing that only you do. It's what makes your heart sing and your blood boil and your body zing. We want to get really clear on what is that one thing you want to bring out. Then, we will dive into how you want to use that thing, your genius, your creation, to make an impact and who is it for. Finding your audience is imperative.

First of all, I will ask you to get two separate journals. These can be yellow legal pads, composition notebooks, pretty journals with affirmations on every page, whatever turns you on that you will spend some time writing in. I've got questions and prompts to get you writing: I call it from the body to the page. One journal will be your gratitude journal; I'll explain in a bit. The other journal will be where you write everything: brain dumping, ideas, lists, and more. I love to get those inexpensive composition notebooks and then spend a bit of time collaging the covers, depending on what that particular notebook is for. Make sure to have some favorite writing utensils, a great pen, colored inks, maybe some neon highlighters or crayons, okay? Now we can begin.

Let's Get Curious

Apparently, you are wanting to change your work situation.

It's time to look at that place, the work, the environment, the people, the time. Can you tell me what you aren't happy about within this current place? Take out one of those journals you got and get ready to write some questions and answers in it. I want to go through some journaling questions with you so you can get down to the truth of the matter. This is so important when you want to make a change, because *why?* Why, why, why? I will sound like a two-year-old!

But we want to know the deep truth, what you feel deep inside, and why you want to make a change.

In that journal, make a list of all the things about your current job you dislike. Think about why you don't like them. The place, the people (your boss and your co-workers), the schedule, the work itself, the money you make from it, the commute, all the things. Look at why you don't like them.

What was it about the job that you liked in the beginning? Why did you take this job? What has changed?

What do you still like about the job now? What does it help you do? Afford you to do? Who do you like? What have you learned from working at this job?

This is a way to look at your current situation, take stock, and turn it into a *gratitude practice!* Yes, by taking a step back from the situation you are not happy with and looking at it with a different perspective, like what good has it done for you, you will start to help you see the truth of what and why are want to make a change.

Gratitude Practice

Let's go there… do you have a gratitude practice? What is gratitude? It's feeling of thankfulness, of feeling blessed, fortunate, of having appreciation for something that pleases and satisfies you. Feeling gratitude makes you feel love and loved, warm and fuzzy.

Gratitude will shift your perspective. It is an affirmation of goodness, and acknowledgement that we have good things. Robert Emmons, a professor at University of California and an expert on gratitude, says that having gratitude helps us see life as a gift. I love that. Life is a gift. He says, "The act of gratitude has been found to greatly and positively influence not just relationships, but one's own emotional status."

Let's get you started with a nightly gratitude practice. You will use the second journal for this writing adventure. Every night before you go to bed, take out this gratitude journal and write in it what you are grateful for this day. Write at least three things that happened that were good for you today. Sometimes, you may wish to keep writing more than three things. Nothing negative goes in this journal; this is only for your words of appreciation.

Example

Today I am grateful for:

- This cozy bed and comforter
- The lovely dinner I had with my husband.
- The morning walk while the sun was rising.
- My new client.
- My new painting because it made me feel so good to start it.

Why do this? It helps you look at your life. Simple. Even if you feel like you have had a shitty day, you can find some good in it. The more you do this practice, the more you look at all the things about your day, your home, your work, your friends, and your life with different eyes. You'll see some things you have taken for granted or maybe have forgotten about. You will observe changes in how you view things in your life, what is good, and perhaps what is not feeding your anymore and what is truly great and ringing your bells!

I have led month-long gratitude challenges where I had my participants write at least ten, and often twenty, items every day of what they were grateful for. Let me tell you, it changes your perspective on many things about your life and some things you get re-excited about and some things you might just want to let go of that are not serving you any longer.

Are you ready to try this? Let's say, do this nightly for one month. Write at least three things, and if you are on a roll, keep adding to that list. You don't have to be a great writer to jot down some thoughts. No pressure on yourself here. Just allow your pen to flow and list those few things every night. You may miss a night here or there, then take a few moments every day to jot down your list. Some folks really like to do this in the morning instead of at night. Find out where your comfortable time for writing them is, but I do prefer at night before bed, because then I can go to sleep feeling really good.

When I do this with my client and ask them to journal with gratitude about their work, like I asked you to list some items earlier about your job, some of them have actually fallen back in love with their job. They have just needed to step back and evaluate what has been going on and perhaps see an easy fix.

Remember what it was that they enjoyed about that work! This may be just what you needed to stay happy at your work place, while you are getting ready to create that bigger change too.

Your Creative Zone of Genius

Now we want to talk about your creative force! What is your artform? What you are wanting to create, change, and step into? Your creative zone of genius. A great book about the zone of genius is *The Big Leap* by Gay Hendricks. He talks about taking your life to the next level: "To give your full attention to that place of satisfaction." Your zone of genius. That's what we want to do too. What are you here for? You are being called to step up and not to live with the status quo; no, not anymore!

Since we are talking about your creative path, I am calling this your creative zone of genius... and when you make that commitment to live in and call upon your creative zone of genius, you spiral higher, with momentum, actions, interactions, and connection to live with your highest power of creativity. Bam!

Creativity and Your Superpower

What is creativity? Another great book I've reread and listened to several times is *Big Magic* by Elizabeth Gilbert. I love how she writes about being creative and what that means. It's about finding inspiration and celebration in living a creative life. She writes about to let go of the suffering and fear and encourages us to dive deep to find the "strange jewels" within each of us. That's what I'm talking about here.

You perceive the world in the way only you know how and how you bring that vision into reality is your superpower. It's about making new connections with new insight. Living a creative life is everyone's right. You are here to live full-on, enjoy your life, and make a statement and an impact. This may be on a smaller level or a huge scale; no matter, no judgement here. But you deserve to live the life you want. Period. I will say this over and over. And now is *your* time, my friend, so let's make that happen.

One thing I want you to remember is that *Thoughts become Words become Things.* This will become your mantra! This is why I will ask you to write, to pay attention to your words, how you talk about yourself, your job, your art, your friends, relationships, etc., and how to ask for what you are wanting. You will see that you will probably change how you describe your life, art, and job by the words you choose to use.

Now it's time for your other journal: *not* your gratitude journal. This is the one you will brain dump in, answer lots of my questions, and see your work and your possibilities unfold!

Exercise: Make That Change

I want you to be aware of the story you keep telling yourself. Remember, only you have the power to change your story. You have the choice. This is a three-part exercise that I learned many years ago from my first coach, Dana Corey, and it is a way to really get down to the truth of a situation. I have used it over and over again with myself and with my clients. I've used different versions of this but this is the way I would like you to proceed. You can use this for all the different things in your life that you are unhappy with and want to change, but for just one story at a time. Again knowing *why* is always the key component to making change.

Step 1

This represents your story now, and is a super powerful exercise, in three different parts. This is time to let it out, be super truthful with yourself. Illuminate yourself up and then shed that skin!

So, Let's focus on one thing you are wanting to change. There may be a few, but just *one* thing.

If you could pick the one thing right now about what is wrong with your job, or what is causing you anxiety, what would it be? What is your main concern today? What would you like to change?

(Example: not having enough money, time for myself, not making time for my own creative work, etc.)

Example: I don't make enough money.

I have a series of statements here and I want you to intersperse your chosen phrase into each statement and then I want you to write your comments, quickly, to that statement. Write not just one comment but several thoughts for each statement.

This is not about being a great writer; there's no need to edit or spell check. I want you to write quickly what comes up for you, a couple of sentences for ea statement. Some of these statements seem redunda.... but they really help get down to the juice inside you, down to the nitty-gritty. This will make you feel like shit at first, but we will change that in step 3 and you will see the light when we are done. I promise!

So grab your other journal and a cup of something, and I want you to fill these out, then we'll move on to steps 2 and 3…

Fill in the blanks with your concern…

1. What makes me angry about (not making enough money, etc.) ____________________ is ____________________.
2. What keeps me up at night worrying about ____________________ is ____________________.
3. What embarrasses me about ________________?
4. The biggest frustration I have about ____________________ is ____________________.
5. What keeps me from moving forward is ____________________.
6. What ____________________ means about me is ____________________.
7. What makes me sad about ____________________ is ____________________.
8. What other people think about me about ____________________ is ____________________.

9. What drives me crazy about ____________________ is ____________________.

10. What I tell myself about ____________________ is ____________________.

11. What I believe about ________________________ is ________________________.

12. What I pretend about ________________________ is ________________________.

13. What I put up with about ____________________ is ____________________.

14. What I don't do about ________________________ is ________________________.

15. Who I blame about ________________________ is ________________________.

16. What I don't have about ____________________ is ____________________.

You can access this sheet from my download files in dropbox. Here is your link: *https://www.dropbox.com/s/6rekk5i6f1d9vjm/Change%20your%20story-%20Make%20That%20Change%20Part%201.pdf?dl=0*

Step 2

Now, look at your story you just wrote to all those statements. You must make a *decision* to change your story! You've got to want to.

Do you see the old story, a pattern, or habit of thinking about the thing your chose to fill in the blanks with? Think about it this way, and you must be very honest with yourself: what is the *cost* of keeping this old story? It feels like crap, right? Misery. How good does that really feel?

What is the *payoff* of staying in this story? What is the payoff of that misery? Do you feel righteous?

Humans want to be right, so what are you getting out of it? Do you want to stay in the same cycle? I call that the *cycle of perpetual sameness.*

Be objective. How long do you want to hang on to this story?

Will you be happy in a year if you still say the same thing? Think about it.

Be ready for a change. Do I hear a Hell Yeah?

Step 3

Now, change those statements, each one, and rearrange the words into what you do want, something positive. Rewrite each one in the affirmative.

Be conscious of what you want to move toward, and state it in the present. "Now I am, or now I have..."

Example:

1. What makes me feel happy about having enough money is ____________________.

You have to *believe* this, so make the new statements believable. You are telling your mind your new truth. You are on your way!

Here they are again…

Change the statements below in your journal. Enjoy the change and vision.

1. What makes me angry about (not making enough money, etc.) ____________________ is ____________________.
2. What keeps me up at night worrying about ____________________ is ____________________.
3. What embarrasses me about ________________.
4. The biggest frustration I have about ____________________ is ____________________.
5. What keeps me from moving forward is ____________________.
6. What ____________________ means about me is ____________________.
7. What makes me sad about ____________________ is ____________________.
8. What other people think about me about ____________________ is ____________________.
9. What drives me crazy about ____________________ is ____________________.

10. What I tell myself about ____________________ is ____________________.

11. What I believe about ________________________ is ________________________.

12. What I pretend about ________________________ is ________________________.

13. What I put up with about ____________________ is ____________________.

14. What I don't do about ________________________ is ________________________.

15. Who I blame about ________________________ is ________________________.

16. What I don't have about ____________________ is ____________________.

This begins the Law of Attraction, giving what you want your good positive juju, putting attention on what you do want (not what you don't want or don't have), and giving your desires focus and energy. Give attention to see and write the change. How do you want things to be different? How do you want to feel? Remember to see it as if is is now, in present time. Thoughts become words and then they do become real things.

Do you feel the shift in your energy, in your body, in your vision when you focus on making a change? See how powerful your words are? Now you can see more of what you've been costing yourself by staying where you have been and how easy it can be to open up to what your possibilities. Super exciting, right?

You can also access this sheet from my download files in dropbox. Here is your link: *https://www.dropbox.com/s/5h7svmijv7d5bxv/Change%20Your%20Story%2C%20Make%20the%20Change%20Parts%20Two%20and%20Three.pdf?dl=0*

Playtime – Journaling Prompts

We'll work more with these ideas as we continue through the book, but you can see and feel how you can use your words to ask for what you want and to change what you don't want any more.

Again, what are you desiring?

You want to run your own business. You want to use your art as your career. You want more freedom. You want to be your own boss. You want to make more money. There may be many reasons for you wanting to make a change.

So, let's make another list in your journal! While you are on a roll, let's take some time to dream to help you start getting more clarity on what you do want. This is playtime for you. We are going to expand on this, but for now, write down:

- What do you want to create?
- What is calling you?
- Why do you want to do this thing you want to do?

- How do you want to work?
- Do you want to travel and work on the road, stay home, have an office?
- What are your big aspirations with your art?
- How will you make money from it, or do you need to?

Feel the words open yourself up. How does it feel to write your dreams down? This is a great habit to build upon. Dreaming and writing those ideas down, although they may change. Now is the time to open up and explore the possibilities. Getting into the journaling habit is going to expand your horizons, my friend! Trust me.

What's Holding you Back?

One of the biggest obstacles I hear from my clients in moving forward with their dreams is fear of the unknown.

There are so many more: fear of change, failure, success, losing, not knowing what to do, stepping outside of the box, staying in the box, flying your freak flag, not making enough money...

What are you afraid of? That list can go on and on, I'm sure.

But I really want to ask you, what is the worst that can happen? When you stop to think about it, what might happen? What could be bad?

I'll tell you a little story about my move to the farm several years ago. I wanted to leave Portland and live in the country, which had been a dream of mine for years. Plus, I was fed up and burnt-out with city life and the pace I was living at that time. I wanted peace and tranquility and nature. My husband, critters, and I picked up and bought fourteen acres of gorgeous land with not much of a formal plan but a strong intuitive pull and desire.

It was fabulous and it was intensely hard work while I was still teaching dance and traveling. It was a dream come true. We got more livestock - eight goats (beautiful pygoras for their beautiful fiber, plus some cutie patootie pygmies), and twenty-one chickens that were so entertaining and adorable (and not for meat!), and we built barns and chicken coops (they were incredible art barns, let me tell you! When Jeff builds something, well… he has a vision!).

We were creating our corner of paradise. Then we opened up a vegetarian wine bar cafe in our little town (which, by the way, had lots of hunters!). Who is the crazy one here? But I believed in my vision and my dreams. We built a little beauty, made delicious veggie food, brought the town's community together, started a farmer's market, educated people about eating good healthy food, drank lots of great wine, and pulled musicians together. I still continued to teach yoga and travel to teach dance too. It was delicious, delightful, and freakin' hard work. The hardest I've ever worked in my life. I loved it. It was what I wanted to experience.

Then we decided to change again. We did it, loved it, and after several years, it was no longer serving us. I had new ideas and desires and visions. So, we packed up, sold everything and moved back to our house in Portland. Something I thought I would never do was move back to my old house there, but we did and it started our next adventure, the next chapter in my life and career as well as ours together. I would do it again, through the tears and sweat and laughter and love. It was a dream and I fulfilled it. I was satisfied. I continue to this day to reinvent myself and my creative adventures.

Nothing is Forever

Because nothing is forever. And you can always make another change. It's that simple. So I ask you again, what is the worst that can happen if you move forward into your dreams? What if you quit your job to paint full time, and then realized you needed a little extra income? Is that the end of the world? No, maybe you get a part-time job until this next class launches or your next art gallery exhibit opens or the new season kicks off for your dance classes. There are so many lovely solutions but often, you don't take the time to look at all the possibilities.

If we cling to only what we know, we become desperate. We feel that desperation in our bones, that fear to make that change and that keeps us in resistance. When you feel desperate, where in your body do you feel that?

What would it feel like to release that resistance? Whew... you can breathe that in now, baby. Feel the shoulders come down, feel the breath deepen, feel the lightness of being.

Make the Decision

You have the choice to stay where you are, whether from fear of change or not knowing what to do. You can make the decision to change, shift, and shake it up. Only you, my friend, can make the decision to step into what you are wanting, desiring to change, to make a difference, to use your creative juices, artistry, skills, knowledge, experience (or even your lack of experience), and vision to create the change you desire to see in yourself, your work, and the word.

"Be the change that you wish
to see in the world."

~ *Mahatma Gandhi* ~

What it comes down to is you stepping up and saying, *"Hell yeah"* to going after what you want. You have to make the choice. You can release the resistance, break down the walls, and move forward. What happens when you decide on the one thing? All the other choices fall away. Really, no more wishy-washy, no more *"but what if's"*, nor more *maybes*. No going back, then, friend; you now have the opportunity to move forward with that intention because you made the decision.

You, and only you, have the choice. You can't put that on anyone else: no blame, no guilt, just the beautiful opportunity to move forward into your desires. To create. What is that for you? To paint, write, teach, dance, cook, flow with freedom and confidence and the knowing that you are stepping up, leaping big into that dream, and that you, can make it happen because you made the choice?

You came to a decision that this is what you wanted to do and you are taking the steps to make it happen. I am here to help you along the way but it is still all about you. This is your vision to change and live your life big and full of beauty and art. You can live this life with abundance, freedom, prosperity, and, most importantly, joy.

I have several businesses and I have made them come into fruition. We are going to make a plan for you with actionable steps for how to move the needle forward in your plan. Self-education is necessary on so many levels.

There are questions on why and how you want to grow and change and create and share. To live the life of your dreams. To be the creatrix that you are. To paint with abandon, to write with flow, to dance like noone is watching. To listen to your heart, your body, your mind, your soul. Because why? This is your life, these things are your creations. You feel good when you express yourself, when you share those bits of beauty and feelings and pain and experience or the questing for what you want, of what is next, what is now, and what is waiting to be created.

Susanna Clark's writes in her song, "Come From the Heart": *"You've got to come from the heart if you want it to work.*" To truly express and create and give from your heart and soul is a gift for all of us.

Exercise: I Am

This is a delicious exercise in owning who you are. I have used this for years with my dancers and clients, and I just adore how this helps you step into your power, your beauty, your vision of yourself, your use of words in the present, and how to take possession of all of your power and amazingness.

So, first, using the words, "I Am," please write the following in your journal:

"I am ____________________."

This blank could be "a woman," "a mother," "a sister," "a lover," "a nurse," "a teacher," etc.; just use some simple words that "define" who you are or perhaps what you do.

Next, let's dive into that, quickly, and open up your heart and soul to who and what you really are today.

"But really, I am ____________________."

As an example, this could be something like "a divine priestess of the dance," "a mover and shaker," "a magic-maker," "a movement instigator," "a writer of inner feelings," etc.

Do you see what I mean and feel the change? Find the new words and ways of describing yourself and own them. Take yourself down deep, further, into who you really are and/or who you desire to be. Make this an every-day exercise for you while you are reading this book.

How fantastic it is to check-in with yourself every day about how you are feeling, how you desire to show up, how you want to shout it out, and how that makes you feel!

"I am..."

"But, really, I am..."

And don't forget your nightly gratitude practice! After all of these thoughts and questions and exercises, end your day with this simple-yet-profound writing practice.

Celebration!

Now, let's celebrate you! With the help of your gratitude practice, take a look at the work you have already done just in this chapter alone! Whoa... this is great stuff. Asking yourself these questions can get you clarity and acknowledging your willingness and desire to move forward into a more fulfilling and satisfying career and life. It's so important to celebrate all that you are, and all the things, big and small... What is a reward for you? A treat? What can you do for yourself, now, to honor yourself at this stage? Do something that feels good, just for yourself.

Journaling and Envisioning Exercise

So, this is what I want you to do now... and we may do this several times, as your ideas may change for ɔu, may get stronger, more clear, may shift, may even isappear. But now I want you to do this envisioning exercise with me. Ready?

This is fun and great to repeat throughout your journey. Over and over again, I want you to envision what you want or, at this point, what you think you want! No judgment. This may shift continuously as we dive in and that's fabulous. You are a creative soul and we are fine-tuning your ideas.

What I want here is your clarity. Your ideas of what could be for you: your words, paintings, studio, business.

You can do this with me here on the page, or go to this link to settle in and listen to my guided visualization I made for you! Click this link: *https://www.dropbox.com/s/yem47377zx71qqg/Envisioning%20exercise%20for%20Book%20%231.mp3?dl=0*

Let's talk about a day in your life ... can you write down what would feel like a great day for you if you had the job of your dreams?

- What time do you wake up?
- What do you do when you wake up?
- What do you eat for breakfast?
- What is your morning self-care routine?
- Where do you go to work? Home? Office? Studio? Library? The park?
- What exactly is the work you are doing?
- Who are your clients?
- How much do you charge?

- How do you have your business accounts set up?
- Who are you working for? Or who is working for you?
- What are you wearing?
- What are you driving?
- Who is representing you?
- What skills do you have?
- What education do you need to acquire?
- How many employees do you have?
- Who is your business coach?
- What networking groups are you involved with?
- *Why* do you want these things?

Yes, so many questions and some repetitions. Why? I want you to think of and look at every aspect of starting your own creative venture. Find what you are desiring right now so you can move forward with success, clarity, and joy.

What fun, right? From gratitude journaling, to making changes, you've plowed backward into what has been and moved forward into what can be. Hard questions, enlightening thoughts, deeper awareness of all your possibilities. Now it's time to set up some new or renewed practices for daily connection - physical, spiritual, and emotional - and how to change your state and set yourself up for everyday success. Onward!

CHAPTER 5

CHANGE YOUR STATE

I choose me
I could have chosen someone else
But it was you
You, my seductress, running through
my body and my veins
You, my muse, cheering me on
You, my hermit, allowing me to forge ahead into
the unknown
and taking others with me
you, my teacher, gifting me with
your gifts
bestowing on me the wisdom
along with intuitive guidance
you, my angel
full of protecting force and loving arms
I chose me
To dance up tall and strong
To listen and follow
My desires

To live my calling
To shine my light...

~ ***Paulette Rees-Denis*** ~

Temple of Love

Because I am a mover and a shaker, I have found the importance of truly being in my body, of loving my body and feeling good in my skin, all the tattooed bits of it! This body has worked hard for me, especially since it has been my main tool for work. As a dancer, this body is my medium, like a painter uses a brush.

Believe me, it has seen its share of abuse, neglect, and injuries besides all the creative love and juicy divine inspiration.

As I have gotten deeper into my practice of spiritual, physical, and emotional connection and as I have gotten older, I also am deeper into self-loving and taking great care of my body, as well as my head and heart! I want to take care of my body and the body is also designed to take care of me. This body is my home. *Your body is truly the only thing you have in life.* I listen to what it wants and it listens to what I want. It is my temple of love.

And your temple of love wants to be loved. It wants to move, shake, quake, and expand. It wants to be juiced up and flow with ease. Self-care now becomes a blissful experience and a time of renewal, rejuvenation, and re-acquaintance with oneself.

Many years ago, I heard a quote that I used to share with my dancers. Not sure where it came from or the exact words, but it was something like this: "*You never want the body to stand in the way of the soul.*"

I love this! Think about being connected on every level and you have something to say, something to express, create, and share. You want that to come from within, from source, from your heart and soul with ease and flow. You don't want obstacles in the way of your creation. You want to feel good so you can create and work with joy and intuitive guidance. You want your body to move with ease and allow you to move forward with intention.

Why would you intentionally stop that flow, that expression? I see it all the time. "Oh, I can't give up bread even though it bloats me," or "Dairy make me ill, but I love cheese," or "It hurts my knees to move and even though I'm a bit overweight, I'll just suffer." Why do you self-sabotage yourself?

So, I'm curious: how do you truly feel in your body? Do you love your body? Do you love being in your body? What happens when you look in the mirror? Do you feel a glorious connection with yourself? Do you feel disconnected? Do you wish to shed a few pounds? Gain a few? Want to get up off the couch and shake it a bit? Do you wear clothes to hide in or do you adorn yourself with delicious colors and jewelry? Live in yoga pants and a baggy t-shirt? Dress to thrive?

Every day, I want to love my body, move with ease, feel and be strong and healthy, vibrant, creative, productive, alive, and lit up.

I constantly talk about self-care. I have daily requirements that I know when I don't take that time, I don't have the best day possible. Every day is a new day, and I want every day to be the best day of my life. It is time for that makeover for you, my friend! You are here because you want to change your career, your vision of your life, and that includes your temple. So, let's start there.

Because you are here to feel good, *bam*... that is all. Your body is the only thing you have, so it's time to reconnect and fall back in love with yourself. You can stand up and shine, show the world your unique individual beauty and the beauty of your creations. You can walk tall and create and run that business with confidence and pride and feeling freakin' fabulous (and be part of the FF club, that's my global club of being Fucking Fabulous)!

As much as I love a good bubble bath or eating a lovely piece of dark chocolate, taking care of oneself goes deeper. Let's start with basic connection.

I have a daily practice which I have done for the past gazillion years! This is what I give every client to start with. It may seem easy to pass over this part of your career change, but this is the most important part. Again, if you aren't happy in your own temple, how can you share what's inside and expect others to believe it, and even to buy it?

Meditate, Percolate, and Dance Break!

I wake up early, like *way* early, usually before my husband, so I can have my personal time to meditate, write, and move my body. There is a beautiful connection of spirit, brain, and body. And boom-chaka, let the day unfold with beauty, power, and intention. I set myself up for success.

My three-part morning practice, here we go, laid out for you. To begin, do you meditate? Do you have a daily practice of sitting in meditation? Why do this? What is meditation?

It's a great buzzword these days and for very good reason. Simply put, meditation is a way to quiet your mind and get a deep connection with yourself, your inner being, source, god, spirit, whatever you call your belief in the universe. Ah, to quiet that chatter in your head, your monkey-mind as some folks call it! Sometimes, there is so much twirling around up there that you don't know which way to turn. Ever had that feeling?

To create from that divine place within comes from creating time to quiet down, listen internally, and stop the chatter so you can hear what's really important: what source has for you. Get clear! Find some bliss.

I'm not here to teach you how to meditate. There are so many great sources, books, online courses, and teachers out there to help you do that. A few I would recommend to you would be any meditation experiences that Oprah and Deepak Chopra put out, just awesome, *www.deepakchopra.com*. I really appreciate Kristoffer Carter's mediation work at *www.thisepiclife.com*. Plus Insight Timer is an invaluable tool and an everyday use for me, *www.insightimer.*

com . I can give you a quick primer on how to get started because I really do want you to develop a daily practice, while you are working with me from this book and if we are to continue this journey later on as well.

There are several ways to meditate and many belief systems too. When I first started to get into my practice, I was doing more moving meditations and would incorporate some ideas of this into my dance classes, which was awesome! I had a hard time sitting still when I first started. Monkey-mind just wanted to move. I have a lot of energy and sitting still was a challenge. I found that quieting the body was as important as quieting my mind. I did some moving meditations to get myself in the zone. I'll share a moving meditation with you in a bit. There are also lots of guided meditations and visualizations where you listen to a guide; all are good. But listening to yourself is where I want to go now.

Let's start by finding a quiet, safe, place to begin your practice. You want to be sitting in a chair or perhaps sitting cross-legged on the floor. Sit up straight, shoulders back, chest open. Just feel connected to your body. Really give yourself a body scan from your toes to the tip of your head. Concentrate on awareness of your body. Notice how you feel.

Close your eyes and start to slow your breath down. Breathe in a deeper breath through your nose and exhale out slowly through your mouth. Feel the breath continue down from your throat to your abdomen, expanding the lungs and your whole torso.

Yum. With each inhale, expand your belly as if you were filling up your belly with breath.

It's amazing sometimes how we forget to breathe deeply and just take our breath for granted and how shallowly we do breathe through most of our day. So, deepen that breath, fill your whole body up with your life force, your chi, your energy. On each exhale, hollow out the belly, push the breath out, and pull your belly back to your spine as you hollow out. Do this several times and just notice your shift, how your energy and focus have changed in just a few minutes. It doesn't take much, really. Just a few minutes of focus and breathing. Internal wellbeing leads to external wellbeing, to feel in harmony, to be in alignment with your true self.

You have just changed your state! Raising your energy, do you feel the pulse of your life? You're having an intimate connection with yourself and your higher power and awakening more of what is inside you, waiting to be released, created, and shared.

Now, do this for longer and feel a deeper connection with yourself. Is your mind wanting to burst and tell you lots of things right now? Oh, that chatter. No judgment on yourself here; this is a practice. One of the ways that really helped me to quiet and get focused was to visualize clouds wafting by in my forehead, that inner eye, often referred to as your sixth chakra. Those clouds helped me quiet down (thanks to Kristopher Carter and his meditation teachings). Another easy method is to listen to what's around you, something quiet and steady, like the hum of the refrigerator or the air conditioner. Some people like music, although I usually find it distracting, or playing a tape of white noise to get to that settled and quiet place. Some chant, which I also love. But let's start simple and get quiet.

I recommend you do this every morning, first thing, and start by setting a timer for five minutes to begin. There are some great phone apps to use too; I use Insight Timer daily. Lengthen that time every couple of days to seven minutes, ten minutes, twelve minutes, and fifteen minutes. I like fifteen minutes for myself because that is a good amount of time I can afford before I move into the next phase of my morning practice. You can sure go longer if it is working for you and if you're feeling delicious and connected!

Next up: *Percolate!*

I'm not talking about coffee! This is about what is brewing inside you, although you might enjoy a cup of joe or tea after you do your meditation! After you get done with your meditation, you then make space inside and you can start to connect with your head, with your thoughts and words. This means more journaling, my friend! Oh, yes, getting into that delicious practice of connecting *from the body to the page*. I follow in the footsteps of Julia Cameron, who wrote *The Artist's Way*, using her technique of the Morning Pages. That means getting that journal out and writing nonstop, every morning, for three pages.

I started this practice myself many moons ago because I wanted to start writing again and develop a new writing practice. Believe me, this has changed my life. This is important. Pay attention.

The idea here is to start journaling, when you get up and begin your morning practice, with a brain dump. This is the time to empty out, clear out the cobwebs, and get rid of the crap that is floating around. You maybe write some to-do lists or even write something as trivial as "I don't know what to write right now" or "this sucks." It's to get connected to your words, your flow, anything that is going on. You will find your flow as you continue.

Sometimes, I do write a to-do list, sometimes a poem flows through me, sometimes I have to write about some ugly confrontation with someone or a lovely connection with a friend or how beautiful the yard looks or the gorgeous sunrise and my cup of coffee. This is the time to be present, time to notice.

This is not a time for editing or for stopping the flow. Keep the finger to the page. I do recommend a pen and paper, your journal, instead of typing into the computer, but you find what works for you. This is a time to write three pages or to go at it if you have the inspiration. I find that once I release some of the negative build up, I have space for creation. You are emptying out to make room for your genius. Once I do that, I open up to receive a download from source, the next fabulous business idea, the next poem, the reminder of what's next for me, and the connection. That sweet, delicious connection with myself, time that I have taken for me, my creations, my life, heart, and soul.

So, while you are getting into the morning mediation habit and the nightly gratitude habit, I want you to start this habit too. I want you to shake things up. This is not the time to be wishy-washy; this is time for you to fully step into your being, your body and your creativity and your purpose and desires. Commitment is wanted!

Part three of this daily process is *your dance break!* Yep, you gotta move.

Okay, can you commit to doing this, along with your meditation routine? Please note how you feel when you are done, daily, weekly, as you proceed and progress. I want to know. I want you to notice too, and feel the shift.

Remember this song? I mentioned this earlier.

Get up offa that thing! by James Brown: "Dance and you'll feel better." Give a listen and stand up. Move it! YouTube link: *https://www.youtube.com/watch?v=1_uNMy20qAI*

And here is another song I can't help but dance to, by Justin Timberlake: "Can't Stop The Feeling." YouTube link: *https://www.youtube.com/watch?v=ru0K8uYEZWw*. Dang, that video makes me so happy!

So you, when is the last time you danced? I mean, really, full-out, shake your groove thang, and put on a glisten? I hear so many women talk about not moving. Not dancing anymore. Lots of excuses – fear, paralysis, embarrassment, age, whatever...

In a Dance with Desire class I taught recently at a university, we did several of the steps I write about in this book, including a free-form, rockin' dance break. A woman, probably around age fifty, announced to the class, as she was glowing and sweating and laughing, that she had not danced like that since her early college days. Wow and what the fuck? This made me incredibly happy that I could help her find that place to dance and enjoy herself, but it also made me so very sad that she had let that part of her slip away. She wasn't enjoying her own rhythm, grooving to whatever tunes rocked her world, or feeling juicy and limber and free-spirited.

I do hear this *all* the time. Not from my bellydance students, although they too get stuck in a familiar pattern of moves and are afraid to break the mold in some sort of free-form dance. So many women have become too busy to take a break, too embarrassed to let go, too afraid someone will laugh at them, too inhibited to show that they "don't know how to dance." They won't allow the beautiful connection with themselves and with others, to go out with friends to dance in a club, or to take a Tribal Grooves or a workout dance class, yoga, or a salsa class, or Zumba, or NIA, or whatever feels good to them.

"Oh, I can't dance, I don't know how to dance, I don't have the time, I have terrible balance, my knees hurt, I'm too fat, etc., etc., etc." I have heard all the excuses.

But what I have also heard is that once my clients start these daily practices, they start to feel so good. Oh my god! Life is changing. It's time to feel uplifted, re-energize the body, be excited to move again, love the music, stretching, breathing, and sweating, and feel more limber and perhaps even sore from moving in ways you haven't before.

I am inviting you to take this challenge too and add some dance breaks to your morning routine. What does this look like? What if you put on a favorite song after your journaling and just started stretching? Or went to the gym and got a trainer? Some peeps hate the gym but I love it! Or maybe take your dog for a vigorous walk for twenty minutes and listen to some tunes? Getting outside is also an important part of this morning set-yourself-up regime. Nature is where it's at. Get outside.

What if you were to join an online yoga or cardio class and worked out for fifteen to sixty minutes from the comfort of your living room? What can you fit in, what type of movement feels good on you? What will energize you and make you happy and ready to take on the rest of the day? Forget this grumpy rolling-out-of-bed-and-rushing-to-the-office stuff.

Here are a few questions to jot down in your journal and answer.

Journaling Prompts

- What makes your body feel good?
- What ways do you enjoy moving?
- What do you love about your body?
- What would you like to change?

- What have you done in the past movement-wise?
- What physical movement have you always wanted to try?

This is your new life. This is how you are going to succeed in your new creative venture. Open yourself up to all of your creative potentials, feel great every day, and make this new life what you have been dreaming of. Set yourself up for success. You are releasing what has been holding you back; you are stepping into more clarity, more freedom, more possibilities.

Three steps for you to begin daily: meditate, percolate, and dance break! Just get started. Sometimes, taking the first step is the hardest part. Once you take that step, even just a baby step, you will feel the shift in your energy and then it becomes easier to move forward. Build your momentum.

You have to make the decision and you commit to making the change.

Answer these again in your journal and see how your answers might be shifting and expanding.

"Today I am ____________________. But really, I am ____________________ (a superhero, a divine priestess, a meditating junkie…). And my superpowers are ____________________."

Today, what are you grateful for?

And how will you celebrate yourself in this new you?

And here you are, falling in love with yourself! Feel it? Feeling good, feeling present. You are energized and in alignment with your truth, creative spirit, and all your opportunities.

So good, so fresh, so revitalizing. You are moving through changes, internally and externally. And yes, gotta love it. Congratulations. It's time to start rewriting your new story.

CHAPTER 6

REWRITE YOUR STORY

In the previous chapters, you got an ah-ha moment of what has been causing you misery about your current job status and perhaps some body and wellness issues too. You are beginning to see how you can make the changes you want and how you can change your story.

Do you see how doing this work that I'm giving you is going to help you access your inner desires and get you reconnected with your whole being? That leads to deeper and juicier creative flow to channel into your desires for your art and your business, and, ultimately, your whole life. Total well-being is the true desire, right?

Designing your work this way is designing the lifestyle you desire and deserve to have. You're rewriting your story.

When I work with my mastermind groups, these are all the components I share to help my clients move the needle forward; in other words, to get clarity and steps for action and then take the actions needed.

Getting in touch with those old stories and relea them, getting clear on the desires, the future, can move into those dreams with positive action and true connection.

Like I say, I mix the woo with the practical for wholeness and wellbeing, inner and outer connections, for truth and opportunities! Remember that every part of the journey is necessary and important and can also help shape and shift all that you are wanting. You are becoming a shapeshifter!

I am going to ask you more questions for you to answer in that beautiful journal full of your dreams and desires. To have exponential and successful growth, you want to have an idea of your destination before you begin or even just a wish for what it is you want to create. We might change the earlier list of what you want; we want to keep defining it and get super-clear.

Let's Use the Clarity Tool!

It's time for some deeper dreaming and opening up to the changes you want. Here are four steps, the Clarity Tool, to look at your situation and dreams:

Step 1: What is your current status? Answer this truthfully. Lay it out.

Step 2: What are your one-year goals?

Step 3: Why are these goals important?

Step 4: What do you need to learn or gather to achieve these goals?

Great! Let's dive deeper into these steps.

Step 1: What

We discussed a part of your status in the last chapter. Can you spell more of this out? What is working and what doesn't work for you? Looking at your daily life, now including your morning additions, how does your day unfold? Your week?

In your journal, you already wrote a bit about what you are creating. What is your art? What do you think you want to do with it? Spend some more time writing about your art and how you would like to use it. Think about how you can grow with it, and how you want to get it out into the world. What is the outcome you are desiring for your people, and for you?

Step 2: Goals

Are you getting a bit clearer on how you want to use your creative skills and art as a career or a side-hustle? What do you see for yourself? Where would you like to be a year from now?

Step 3: Let's Talk about the Why

This is the most important question of all time! Why do you do what you do? Why do you want to make art, dance, paint, sing, write?

For me, I teach and coach because I love to have an impact. I desire for all beings to live with joy and adventure, passion and connection. We crave connection, as I talked about earlier in Tony Robbins Six Human Needs. As humans, it is inherent in us to live in community. I knew from early on that I was to be a teacher, but not a traditional one. I studied and moved and experimented with so many lifestyles and jobs and artforms from a young age. I was always dancing and making music, art, and writing. I ventured into the healing arts, became a massage therapist, studied tarot, magic, and other healing modalities. While I held regular jobs like being an agent for models in NYC or managing retail businesses, I always had side-hustles. I played in and managed rock bands and performing groups while running my healing business and doing freelance photography. Even bartending on the weekend. I wanted to learn so much, with an undergrad business degree, a bachelor degree in photography, and eventually as I turned fifty, I got my Master's in Writing and Publishing (another dream of mine done!). I started my own publishing company too. As I mentioned before, I had always wanted to have a wine bar so my husband and I took an opportunity and opened a vegetarian wine cafe for a short time, which turned out to be hugely rewarding, great fun, and tons of work. In between the years, I opened my own gorgeous and successful dance studio, while developing and trademarking two of my own wildly sought after dance styles. This led me to traveling the world teaching and performing, publishing musical CDs and DVDs and online classes. I have continued to grow that business to include training and certifying teachers and master teachers in this style. These were all dreams and inspired actions, and I moved into them, even with some uncertainty, knowing that I can always change again.

From early on, I wanted to show that you can be different, and be successful. I did not follow any business book, stubbornly often, and I sure did not do things the traditional way. I made up my own rules and went after what I wanted. Rebel! Sure, mistakes along the way, on many levels, but I had things to share, to teach.

My idealistic desire back in my early bellydance career was that I wanted to bring women of the world together, to empower them and help them find their own creative soul. I wanted to help them build their dream business and do things that felt so good, in the body, mind, and spirit! To beautify their world. And make a change by empowering each and everyone to stand up and be counted. Then, bam, it all happened. I did bring women together and still do. And that is why I love the work I do. I am making a change that makes a difference in someone's life. I am helping to facilitate change, in one person, which leads to another, and to another. This has led to my global retreats, the gatherings in many forms. This is rewarding and powerful work that I have created and envisioned for myself, and sometimes not even knowing what would come next.

Now I have my freedom and I continue to create my own art. I have built my income around all of these creative adventures. I have been my own boss now for thirty years. I wanted to do it my way, I wanted to live life on my own terms.

But I will tell you, that I was stubborn, and yes, I did make mistakes, sometimes in business and money dealings, I have lost lots of money. In fact I almost lost my house once. I have hurt people along the way, and been hurt. I have miscommunicated, probably burning a few bridges, for different reasons. Lots of things have gone wrong, but more things have gone right, especially now. I started to pay more attention to how I did my business, and decided to ask for help. Damn, that was hard for me. But I realized I don't know it all. And others do have ways to help. Getting a coach was one of the best moves I could make. Opened up my eyes to all the possibilities. Plus becoming more attuned to myself, inner connection and well being, listening to my inner guides, and finding out what was next. I had to let go of the reins a bit, and find out what I could really do as a business woman, creatrix, and use my creative skills in better ways to help me grow in all the ways. And that is why I am so adamant about helping you.

You don't have to do it alone. I"ve got you, my friend, and let's do this so you don't have to make the same mistakes I did. I am living my dream and making a difference. That is my why!

What is *your* why?

Simon Sinek says, "People don't buy what you do, they buy why you do it!" I love that statement. Can you feel the passion, the heart and soul in certain creations? Don't you want your work to touch someone? To give back to the world? To give a spark of joy, or a feeling of love, or cause for conversation, or ease in doing something else? What do you want your work to do and why?

Exercise: 7 Levels Deep

Here is another exercise I want to share with you. I first learned to use this with my further studies through Tony Robbins and with Dean Graziosi. Amazing coaches! This will help clarify for you what drives you to create, what motivates you to accomplish what you are wanting. Grab that journal and get to answering these questions for yourself!

- What is important to you about becoming successful?
- Why is it important for you to ______________________?
- Why is it important for you to ______________________?
- Why is it important for you to ______________________?
- Why is it important for you to ______________________?
- Why is it important for you to ______________________?
- Why is it important for you to ______________________?

Fill in those blanks!

Example:

- What is important to you about becoming successful? *I want to make more money.*

- Why is it important to you to make more money? *To raise myself up and release the anxiety*
- Why is it important for you to to raise myself up and release the anxiety? *So I can live with more ease and freedom*
- Why is it important for you to live with more ease and freedom? *So I can tune into what is next for me and live to my fullest potential.*
- Why is it important for you to tune into what is next for me and live to my fullest potential? *So I can continue to grow my business and my personal life.*
- Why is it important for you to continue to grow my business and my personal life? *So I can reach more people and make a change in the world.*
- Why is it important for you to can reach more people and make a change in the world? *Then I know I am making a difference*

Seven levels of why, my friend. Can you feel it? How does this affect the way you are looking at what you are wanting? Does it make it clearer and even more important?

Step 4: What do you need?

What do you think will help you to move forward? What are you wanting to add to your own toolbox of actions and desires? We are going to get into more practical steps coming up soon, but like I said, I mix the woo with the practical! I'm not quite done with the woo!

CMO: Creative Mode of Operation

Do you know what I mean when I say woo? Or woo-woo? This is the spiritual side of life. We all desire to have that connection with ourselves, our spirit, body, and mind; that is why I continue to take you through these steps and questions, often more than once. Getting clearer and clearer on what you want, how you are feeling, how your body feels, and getting those crazy thoughts out of your head. These help to get you out of overwhelm and into your creative mode of operation. Just call this your CMO! To know your why helps you to get into your what, and what's next, and how to, and who to, also. This includes laying down your actionable steps, learning and understanding who your ideal customer avatar is, realizing your true purpose, and, above all else, feeling great! This combines all the woo with structure and stability, being connected to your higher self, inner self, god, with some logical organization to that you CAN make it happen! And to learning how you work best, what does and does not work for you. You will be gaining you new skills and operational techniques to allow all that ease and flow, that inspired place of creation and fulfillment. All to come...

Future Tripping

We have done some envisioning earlier in the book. Now I want to take that a step further into what I call Future Tripping. I like to do this as a guided meditation. This is taking you into your future so you can create that future of your dreams. Remember, only you can create what you want. Read through the exercise and then give yourself some time for this meditation on your future self.

I'm attaching a link for you, so I can talk you through this, as a guided visualization! So fun…Click here to download. (Song is Omar, by Gypsy Caravan) *https://www.dropbox.com/s/mmdagnvekdgn1u7/Future%20tripping%20for%20the%20book.mp3?dl=0*

Sit or lay down in a quiet comfortable place where you won't be disturbed and turn off that cell phone. Close your eyes. Slow and deepen your breath, filling yourself up with a deep breath, expanding the belly, and slow the exhale as you hollow out that breath. Breathe in; breathe out. Feel the body relaxing, being held by the earth, the chair, the floor. Allow the body to soften and sink into relaxation, legs uncrossed, arms by your sides or in your lap. Release the shoulders. Feel the deep pulse of your breath as you focus on that breath.

Let's visualize. In your mind's eye, you see a light in the distance, perhaps a dancing bubble of light. It is swaying as if dancing and slowly coming closer to you. In that light is a person. A person full of vitality, you can feel it emanating from her. Full of joy. You realize that person looks like you, yet different.

That bubble of light is in the future, and holding the future you within. Take a look at yourself, there, in the future. How do you look? What is different? What has changed?

What are you wearing? How are you moving? Can you talk to yourself? Ask your future self what she is doing. How she is doing. She is powerful; she is living your dream; she is successful and juicy and colorful. Ask her what she wants to tell you. Ask her what you need to know now to move forward, what will lift you up to keep stepping into your CMO. "You've got this," she says. "We've got this." As she moves and dances closer to you, you can feel the love and the inspiration and all your opportunities knocking on your door. You can feel yourself expanding out to reach her and she gets closer and closer. You reach out to pull her into you, to bring all the possibilities and all the successes and all the wellbeing into you. Because your dreams are here.

As you bring this energy into you, feel a shift in your heart, your energy, your body. Feel the pulse of excitement and creative adventures as you create your future as you want it to be. Return to your breath and your body as you stretch and twist, keeping your eyes closed. Slowly rise and stretch.

Embody that feeling. Dance with that image of you, that feeling. Move your body as you breathe in that image and feeling. Sway and bend, shake and roll, stretch and twist. Inhale. Breathe in; breathe out. Feel the goodness of that desire and that it already is. Notice how it feels in you. Notice where in your body you feel it. In your heart? In your belly? Your throat?

Allow it to expand and fill you up, into every limb and joint and pore. Own it.

You may take a few more minutes to write in your journal your experience and any messages you received from your future self.

Thoughts become words become things! When you do this type of exercise, your brain doesn't know fact from fiction. If you picture this as if it's already done for you, your brain says, "Hell yeah, this is how it is."

Then you draw it into you. Manifestation! You start to embody that new thing, the new job, the new body, the new money, the new you. You want to feel it inside.

This is your time to really focus on how you want your life to look, how you want your work to be for you, how you see your days, your weeks, your months, a year from now, or even longer. How you feel, what you are wearing, where you are in the world, what your office looks like, who is working for you, where are you living, etc. Details! You can create what you want. The universe has it ready for you when you ask. The more you see it, the more you believe it. And as Wayne Dyer said, "The more you believe it, the more you see it!" You've got to believe it first, that this can really be your life! It feels so empowering to know that you can make the changes you desire, to get clarity, and to feel it in your body. Embody those desires not just in your mind and heart, but in your body too.

This is how you rewrite your story. Your past is over. This is your time now, be the chameleon. Be the shapeshifter. Change that story to this new you. You must commit to this desire. Set your intentions. Commit it to yourself. Believe it; only you can make the choice to change. Move and dance forward with those intentions from your heart. Stand up and walk with pride!

How was that for you? Is it becoming easier to see what you are wanting? Is it becoming believable for you? Clearer? How does it make you feel? Excited/motivated? Ready to take action?

Tell me, my beautiful one, who are you today?

"I am ________________________. And I know my work matters because ______________________."

And today, what are you grateful for? What will you celebrate these beautiful revelations? You are so worth it! And here is another life short Iwrote about future tripping! Changing your story to make it easy, doable, and moving into all that you can be, down deep in your heart. Enjoy the journey.

FUTURE-TRIPPING INTO BEING-NESS

Paulette Rees-Denis

Not to give in to the
Plethora of abundance
The seduction of hedonism
The congratulations of the reward
She invests in herself
Knowing what's to come
Changing her story to make it easy
Ah, ease...
Changing her words for the support
Not the backlash
With the-but if she does, the I do's, the judgement
calls
Shaking and shivering, trembling
With her deep knowing of what she can have
Of what she desires
Future-tripping into being-ness
Seeing her dreams as the future
Already past
With fury she tosses out the cakes and the bottles
and the I don't cares
The I love my body this way's
To truly go after what she knows
Deep down in her heart...

CHAPTER 7

YOUR MONEY GAME

THIS IS THE SUBJECT that most women and some men are afraid to talk about: money!

I always hear the song from one of my favorite movies, Cabaret, with Joel Grey and Liza Minelli... *"Money makes the world go 'round, the world go 'round, the world go 'round!"* YouTube link: *https://www.youtube.com/watch?v=PIAXG_QcQNU*

Let's you and I talk about money. I am curious about your money story. We all have old money stories. Earlier we talked about some of your old stories, releasing them, and rewriting them. Now it's time to deal with your money. And what money you are wanting, and what stories here you can change too.

Earlier on in my careers, I made money but I never paid attention to it. Just bringing it in and sending it back out again. It had a good flow. But even though I always wanted to know more about my money and how to save it or invest it or even make more, I still did not focus on it. For whatever reasons, I did not take money and investing, or saving, too seriously. I just wanted to create and live my life with freedom. Not understanding that with money I could create even more freedom and more creating. I was making enough to survive and more and building my business. And that was just fine.

There was a time when I had my dance studio that women would be taking several classes a week and buying things in my retail shop, which was awesome and exciting. It was a great community center with lots of delicious offerings for my students. They would laughingly, sometimes begrudgingly, hand me check after check and say they were giving all their money to me, as they decked themselves out with the goods in my shop, and took the classes, and flourished. Even though those checks had my business name on it, they thought it was to me personally. Indirectly, yes, but that business cost a small fortune to run. I would laughingly say to them, "Ha! Not me, love, I don't see this money!"

Those comments to me started making me feel guilty about taking their money. I started developing a complex about accepting their money, asking for payments. I wanted to keep my pricing low so everyone could afford to come and dance and I was always finding ways to discount classes or products. I felt like they had no idea what it cost to run a brick-and-mortar business. This may or may not have been true but it's what I was thinking. I became more and more afraid of making money. This was my story I made up and it made me crazy stupid. How twisted it that, right? Eventually, that hurt part of my business at that time.

My stories became, "I can't make money with dance. There is no money in teaching dance. I can't make money with my art."

I worked until I burnt myself out. I did not know how to handle money, pay off debt, or invest. Finally, I chose to go away to heal different parts of me, including these ridiculous money stories. It took a while. Years later, I finally know better.

What are some of the money stories you keep telling yourself?

Remember, words are strong influencers in your brain. This is what I continue to hear from women who want to work with me: "I can't afford it; I don't make enough money. I'll never make money from this. I'm broke. I'll never get to live that dream. Maybe next year."

Do you hear that in you? Do you say these things?

This is what I want to tell you: money is empowering. Money is energy. It's an exchange. There is a beautiful money flow when you change your story, tell your story, and allow yourself to receive. You are made for shining your light. Illumination! You want more; you want better. It can happen. You can ask for money, for *more* money to live the life you want, have a successful career, and be wealthy. I mean wealthy on all of the levels: spiritually, physically, and emotionally.

It is not selfish to want more money nor is it shameful to make money from your art. I say this so often and teach my teachers-to-be and my clients that they can build their dreams to sustain them in such a beautiful way. It is not greedy, selfish, or wrong to ask for more money. You have taken the time to invest in yourself and your creative career, and you deserve all you desire. Build your lifestyle how you want it.

I had a client once who did not even want to talk about money, either the money she was making or the money she was to pay me for my services. Waiting until the very last minute to settle up on payment with me was her MO and it was frustrating for both of us. She did not want to figure it out. Of course, we looked at the situation in-depth, as we had to, and she was realized she had to do the money work if she wanted to grow and prosper as well. She was ready to face her fears. In reality, she had a successful outcome, and income. We talked and went through options and possibilities for her to change that story. She rewrote her story! She released those old stories she had of feeling guilty making money as a woman creative entrepreneur. Yes, she can make money from her creations. Now, she continues to invest in herself and her career. She has even quit her side job to continue to build her dream job and is making money and loving it.

First, change your mindset about the money you are making now. Go to your gratitude practice and look at what you have, what that money has afforded you. This will give you a better perspective on your income. Once upon a time, I said those words, the same old story over and over again, even when they weren't true anymore. The story of never being able to make enough money off of what I do. When I was sick of that story, I made the decision to change my mindset, my words, and rewrite that part of my life.

Then it was like the clouds parted and I could feel the release of the resistance around money and life in general.

There's a lot of ways to make money and there are many things you can do with your money when you make it.

It is a great thing for you to make money from your art. There is enough money in the world to go around. You deserve it. Look at your skills, desires, and talent. The time and money you have spent to gather tools, learn the trade, take classes… all this is investment in your self-improvement. You are meant to be wealthy and share your heart.

Not having enough money creates more anxiety, fear, and tension in all that you are and do. Do you want to live in that perpetual cycle of sameness, not moving forward for the fear that is holding you back from achieving your dream? From making more money and expanding all your possibilities?

What if you turn those phrases from up above around?

"I can't afford it" to "I can afford it" or "I am going to afford this soon" or "I choose to afford this." "I don't make enough money" to "I make good money" or "I make enough money" or "I'm on my way to making more money."

Don't you feel a different energy when you change the way you say things and change your mindset around it? Words are powerful and so are your beliefs.

Mindset: it's what you believe about yourself.

The "Try" Word

Here's another word to distinguish from your vocabulary. Try. as in, "I'll *try* to change" or "I'll *try* to come to class."

People! There is no "try." You either do or you don't. Try is noncommittal. Try is ho-hum. There is no forward energy in using that word. Don't you want the things you do to be a hell yeah, or even a hell no? Feel that in your gut. "Yes, I want to do this" or "No, I don't." That's your choice.

You want to make money from your passion, make the life you are meant to live, and create what makes a difference in the world

When (not *if*) you decide you are going to change your mind, you can. You commit to yourself. Doesn't that feel good? That committing feels like a super powerful form of self-care. Another act of self-love. You can do anything if you believe it and ask for it..

What do you charge?

Time to think about what you charge! This is a biggie. So many times I have heard my clients say that they want to reach everyone, or that they want to check out the competition. Well, friend, it is worthy to see what the current pricing is for what you are offering, But you also want to look at your time and investments and all the back end pricing that goes into your product, your gift, your class. Because no one else is you, and no one gives how you give.

Oh boy… are you going to give your work away? Maybe you have been giving your art away or teaching a free class or charging a small amount just to pay the rent for your space. You're afraid to ask for more. You're looking at your "competition." You want others to afford it and you don't think they will pay more for your work or your class.

It's time to step up, my friend. You want to make this work, right? You are serious about making this career change and making your business successful. Move into a category that is only about you, and your specialty, and your superpowers. Become a money magnet and draw it to you… this is not selfish, or foolish, your people are waiting for you. This is just a raindrop of possibilities here and I could write a whole book about money, but others already have, so I have some recommendations for you at the end of this chapter.

Your ICA

Who is your ideal customer avatar (ICA)?

Your ICA is your perfect customer, the one who your work speaks to, the one who wants what you do. This is important in the big picture of being monetarily successful. You want to think about a few things here: what does your art give to the world? How does it affect the buyer? What is the purpose of creating your work? What are you saying to the world? What change do you want to see in your ideal customer? What change to they want to see? Who will buy your work? Really, ultimately, it is about their outcome. What is their result?

This is an important discovery as you venture into entrepreneurship! You really want to know who your target audience is! This is your ICA. When you know who that is, then you know who to reach out to not only who you make your work for, but also who to advertise and market your work to. Who is your consumer? Why do they want it? What will it do for them?

I ask this of my clients all the time. The initial response is usually looking at me like I'm nuts: "Well, of course I want everyone to buy my art, or take my classes, or read my book." But no, that is not the case. You have strengths that touch some people. You have a style that attracts certain folks. You have things to say to a certain group of people.

If you felt like you really wanted to reach out and teach high school students how to write poetry in an after-school class because you have so much to offer these young adults having raised three children yourself, then you wouldn't advertise in *Vogue Magazine*. You would look to advertise in the school newspaper or a local zine or at the local after-school hangout. You'd target them with Facebook or Instagram ads.

If you wanted to teach art to mothers with small children because you were once in that place and you know how great it was to have a class with other like-minded women in the same situation, then you would market your art classes at possibly local coffee shops or young children's clothing stores.

I had a dance teacher-to-be say she wanted to teach all women, feeling very all-inclusive and idealistic. When I asked about her strengths as a teacher, what she loved about teaching, what kind of music she would use in class, where she would teach, etc., it turned out that she loved techy-world-type hip hop music and wanted to teach in a high-impact and high-energy style. Great, but would an older women who wants to dance easy and slow come to her classes? Probably not. She would want to target a younger audience that loves that kind of music and who want a super hard-core dance workout and she could figure out where to find them in her area.

You want to know what exactly you are offering, how you are offering it, what format you are using to know who will love this format, and what kind of creative business woman you are so you know who will love what you are offering. Who will be attracted to what you are doing so they get what they are wanting from it? Why you are offering this thing... are you solving a problem for your customer? What is the end result for your people? And why are you doing it?

Remember what Simon said: "*People don't buy what you do, they buy why you do it.*"

It's important to know why you are doing this thing and that leads to knowing who your ICA is so you know the words to use when you are writing up your copy or course description. You want to know who she is, where she lives, where she hangs out, what her interests are, even perhaps what she wears and where she eats depending on what you are selling or preparing.

Take some time now and write in your journal who that client is. Tell yourself all about her.

Proximity Is Power!

And this is a great time to talk about who you surround yourself with! They say that the five people you must surround yourself with are where you are in the world. If you surround yourself with negative people who are constantly bitching or people who are constantly broke then likely you will fall into that category too. If your five besties are in dead-end jobs or unhappy with their lives and they are content to stay there, then how will you move up? Many people like to pull others back down because they want co-dependency; if they are suffering they want everyone to suffer. Do you know anyone like that, who likes to place blame on anyone and not taking initiative to make that change themselves?

But you are different and you are ready.

If you surround yourself with powerhouse creatives who are making change and building their dream careers and lives, then won't you feel that incredible energy? That desire and passion, that inspiration and momentum? I suggest you can find a mastermind group or a networking group to help you and hold you accountable for your moving up in your life! And always, hiring a mentor or a coach to keep you on track and guide you into more ways than you knew possible is always on top of my list. You can surround yourself with your perfect customers too.

Proximity is power. Be with people who will uplift you. *You* be an up-lifter too! There are people waiting for you… believe it and see it and do it. Gather with those like-minded entrepreneurs and customers and support each other and you will feel a shift in your energy, your art, and your life!

"Today I am ______________________________."
Write about being a badass money making machine! Say it out loud while you are looking in the mirror! When you say it outloud it takes on a different resoncance in your body. You embody it. I want you to own it, and mean it when you say it outloud. Wowza. Make it a mantra. Every day, twenty times a day. *I am a badass dancing money magnet!*

Celebration… how will you celebrate your new money?

How does it feel to identify and release those money stories. You can do the Make the Change exercise around money, too. We want to stand up and feel good about making money, showing others that money is good and our right, that we have worked for it and desire to live with it, and also help others with it. You not only boost yourself up, but inspire other women, other people, perhaps in your own chosen creative field, that they too, can live with prosperity and really make a living off of their desired career path. And how cool is that?

Next we get into some practical methodology th
will help you really make all of your inspired ideas and
dreams work for you.

Resources

1. *Think and Grow* Rich by Napoleon Hill
2. *You Are a Badass at Making Money* by Jen Sincero
3. *I Will Teach You To Be Rich* by Ramit Sethi
4. Financial advisors: *My Financial Girlfriend*, *https://www.facebook.com/myfinancialgf/*

CHAPTER 8

MAKING YOUR MAGIC ACTION PLAN

"Attention energizes, intention focuses."

~ ***Deepak Chopra*** ~

Inspired by Deepak Chopra's quote above, I added what must happen, and that is taking action to get results! *Attention energizes, intention focuses, action equals results*! Everyone has some sort of way they get things done! This may or may not be a successful practice for you. Do you fall into overwhelm when you look at your to-do lists? Your piles? Dang, those piles! What is your creative mode of operation for making stuff happen? Are you super anal and have a strict structure that can't be broken? Does that make it hard to be spontaneous for a free moment or a good time? Or are you a free spirit and just hope that you will remember to get it done? Maybe you love deadlines but wait until the last minute and then sweat it because you may not make the deadline? is that working out for you?

As you start and continue on this new, creative adventure for yourself, you will brainstorm and write down many lists of potential things to get done. From registering new business licenses to new business cards and designing logos, adding Facebook and Instagram pages, building websites, gathering email lists, joining networking groups, besides actually doing the creative creating – those lists… oh my goddess!

Definitely some items are more mundane than others but you still want them to get done. I want to show you a way that will make those steps way more enjoyable and allow you to work with ease and use your time more efficiently. That is still the ultimate goal, right?

Keep remembering that future you and see that already done. You are already living the life of your dreams. You are feeling great in your temple, honoring your body, connecting with your inner self, finding time to create and enjoy while you are lining up the work, the clients, the income, and having a great time! Keep that picture up and running… feel it and believe it.

Vision Boarding

Have you ever made a vision board? A vision board is a place, it could be a piece of paper, journal, or posterboard, where you place images and words of what you are envisioning. A dream board, a visual wish list. Now would be a great time for you to make one.

I'm always cutting out photos or words from old magazines and newspapers before I recycle them and either saving them for a collage or pasting them in my journals of dreams and desires and beautiful places, people, things that turn me on. Perhaps a new place to visit, or a book that moves me, or an inspired quote, what ever is calling me at that time, for that desire.

When you start to collect images, you want to feel the desire in your gut, in your heart! Know that it's for you, that you can have it, that it is waiting for you. The universe has your back. This is a great way to keep on building on your dreams, making them more profound. You know what you want, where you'd like to go, who you want to surround yourself with, and these images and words give your dreams more of a concrete vision.

I find big sheets of paper work best because they gives you more space to dream on. Gather up some large paper, glue, scissors, and old magazines you don't want to keep and start going through them looking for words or phrases of what looks delightful and delicious to you and how you want to feel. Look for images of people, clothing, places, cars, or colors of how you want to look, feel, see, wake up to everyday, visit, etc. Classrooms of people, stacks of books, fabulous clothes, meals, dollar bills, a gorgeous house, whatever feels like the bounty treasure to you.

Paste and collage and overlay, however the images speak to you. You don't have to worry about making it an incredible art piece and don't edit yourself if you are pulled toward an image or word. Grab and cut or tear and paste! Make a vision board that is screaming out about you. Put it around your workspace or house, wherever you will see it every day and allow yourself to feel what that feels like when you have it. Take a picture of it and share it on social media. Hold yourself accountable. Then consider it already done and bask in that glory of your success. You might make several of these as part of your daily journaling or creative process, maybe some mini cards, like an oracle deck to carry with you, whatever. Get uber creative and have fun with your visions, goals, and possibilities!

Your Magic Action Plan

"Where you focus goes, your energy flows."

*~ **Tony Robbins** ~*

On to the lists.

Now you are making your to-do lists. How many times have you made one and then gone into overwhelm? Do you start multitasking in order to get things done? How well are they getting done, when you are feeling pulled in a zillion different directions? Are you feeling stressed just thinking about them?

When this has happened to me in the past, I usually sat on the floor in the middle of my living room and cried! Well, that sure didn't get me anywhere except wanting to run away and then never get anything done!

There are lots of ways to change this feeling in your body and heart, as we've talked about. First, you want to change your state. If you continue to "try" to accomplish something and you are feeling so much resistance, then what will happen? It may turn out like shit, it might not get done right, your good intentions and love won't be infused in it, and you may climb further into that black hole.

So, step away, take a nap, take the dogs out, go for a run, take a yoga class, meditate, dance break, until you feel better and then you can come back to it with a fresh head, an energized body, and a new start.

I'll show you a great method for creating a new way of listing those to-dos so that they become way more exciting, approachable and doable. This is what I call your *Magic Action Plan* (MAP). You can follow a road map, a treasure map, a path to get you to the next step, the next level. Think of it as taking you to your treasures, riches, or pot of gold at the end of the rainbow!

Get your journal out, capture your ideas, and start making your new list of to-dos for getting your exciting creative business started and growing. Start with you morning practices, and think about what you want for this new creative adventure. What are the practical items that will get you started and moving on? I mentioned some above, like your business name and licensing, new biz cards, hiring a website designer, creative time, phone calls, writing your new bio. You can keep you household items separate as we get started, but you'll see your how daily life will flourish with this practice!

Next, start to prioritize them. What needs to happen first? What must get done before something else can get done? Which one is the fun creative one?

For today, pick your top ten for your business. In your journal or on a fresh sheet of paper, make three vertical columns, drawing a line down from top to bottom.

Your first column will be your actionable items: what are you wanting to get done?

Your second column is your results. If you do this thing in column one, what will happen? What is the end result? How will this grow your desires, your business?

Your third column is your purpose for doing this thing! Not just the result, but *why* do you want this done? How will it make you feel? How will it make your life and business better? This could be because you want it to feel good and make a difference or make an impact on your life and your business or bring you a weekly paycheck. Know your why!

That sounds pretty simple and it is once you get into that groove and do this a few times. It puts all your to-dos into perspective and makes them so doable! Gives you the purpose behind the action and makes your heart happy. Because you know what you want to do, and then finding out the deeper purpose behind the actions… makes so much more sense, doesn't it?

One more step you can do is to *chunk that list down.* Put some of the like items together and do them at the same time. This is a very productive way to get more done in shorter amounts of time. Here is an example: you want to make several phone calls. Schedule in a time and a day to make the calls and do them all at one time, and see how fast they get done.

There, bam, on to something else! This is a great use of your time and very effective to help get things done. You'll notice that the items you thought would take so long or were unmanageable or that you never had time for will get done with ease! You are out of overwhelm! Not only have you saved time, but look at how well they did get done because you know the result and you have a deeper purpose. And celebrate that!

Balance

You listed some business items but there are other things you must do. You want to add in your daily and weekly non-work related things because you do more than work! You have a rich and full life and you want to stay in balance.

Perhaps you have a family and you need to pick up your daughter at school every day at 3 p.m. You want to go to the grocery store because you need to eat. You want to schedule in a lunch date with your girlfriend because you want to have some fun and she inspires you or take that dance class to get that body moving. Why? Because it will make you feel energized and connected with your body too. On the MAP, you want to put in your daily life with your whys so that you keep that balance and move the needle forward with intention.

Here is one example: My action: going to a dance class, the result: feeling fit, and my purpose: I will love my body more.

When you start running your own business, it is easy to fall into working all the time, especially because now your work is your heart and soul and it's fun! I worked 24/7 for so many years, partially because I thought I was supposed to and partially because I was very driven and type-A, but also because I loved my work. This caused imbalance in my relationships, my emotional being, and also my creativity after a while. For some reason, I was out to prove that as an artist and a business owner, having my own business was hard. That was an old story. Eventually I had to step away from burnout and stress.

I was able to turn that story around and come out with my pot of gold, but it took some deconstructing and learning all these lessons to make my life. You don't have to do it the hard way. You have an amazing opportunity unfolding for you now. You get to write your story and make your MAP with clarity, ease, and fun.

Fun and Adventure

Remember to take that down time. Schedule it in and put it on you MAP. Keep to your daily practices and add in some daily, weekly, monthly, and yearly adventures. You are creating what you have been desiring! You have the creative freedom to make it exactly how you want it to be.

When you add in the new things, like friends gathering, art dates, road trips, hikes, workouts, and retreats, you are upping your game. You are adding to the creative juice in your life. Stepping away, whether that be an hour or a week, not only gives you perspective on what you are and can be doing, but it also adds thrills and chills and a new vision.

Ideally, this MAP will help you manage your life with pleasure and will not just feel like just a list. Create every day magic in your life, full of delight, success, and feeling good on this journey. Remember, this is your treasure map and it will bring you to your pot of gold.

Think of it this way: you are now turning your attention to what you what to have happen, what wants to be done. Excellent. These new tools help to energize you, and get you shifting and thinking. Then you set your intention, focusing in on your new thing, pointedly, with desire and motivation because you really want to do this thing. You take easy action with purpose and bam, that creates the results you are wanting to have. Unfolding with ease. There you go. You are welcome!

So, "Today, I am ______________________. Not only am I fabulous and a divine goddess (or whatever you are feeling today!), but I just am. (Fully present and here! Wowza…)

I am so grateful for ______________________."

Let's celebrate you and that MAP of yours. Here is to your organizing and unfolding.

CHAPTER 9

THE ART OF SHOWING UP

Because you want to break those chains that are tying you down
Because you want to be connected with every part of your being
Because you know there is more
Because your heart and soul are bursting with the knowing there is more
Because you want to make an impact in the world
Because you want to live with passion and creativity everyday
Because you want to shine your light
Because you want to fly your freak flag
Because you want to make more money
Because you have always dreamed of having your own business and being your own boss
Because you want your career to be full of joy and abundance
Because you want to live with freedom as well as financial security!

Because you want to live lit up every day
Because you want to feel fucking fabulous

~ *Paulette Rees-Denis* ~

The Art of Asking

There are a lot of "Arts" in living! The Art of being in your body and being present, the Art of creating, the Art of showing up! Because life is a constant creation, and it's yours, the way you want it. You've been laying lots of good ground work. Asking for what you want is HUGE! Not only to get clarity on what you are truly wanting, but then to stand up and ask for it, to say this is what I want. And of course, knowing all the action steps, the results, and your purpose will help you feel confident and sure of what you do want.

By now, you get the gist of what it means to ask for what you want from your heart and soul and body. How to clarify, to speak up with sincerity, knowledge, trust, and the knowing of what you are truly wanting. Of wanting to change, step into, create that desire to make the life you want. You've spent time learning the how to and then doing your meditating, journaling, moving that body, writing and rewriting your dreams, rejuvenating, renewing, and mapping it out, including all the whys, the hows, and the whens.

When you stand up and ask for what you are wanting, can you feel the release of resistance as you feel the deliciousness of deliberately creating? You will never stop thinking and creating, so you can write your story with beautiful deliberation.

To be in alignment with what you are truly desiring is the best feeling. Intuitively knowing it's right with no second-guessing. No more edits! Seeing it in all its glory! Feeling in your gut, in your power center, in your womb, what is right for you, what is now for you, what you are wanting to create to make an impact, to make a difference in someone's life, to share your heart and soul. To spread your art and love.

Do you feel it? You want to allow the flow… you want to go *downriver*, my friend. Not to paddle against the rapids, not to fight the current, but to go with that flow. Why would you want to backtrack, or back paddle, and make it hard? Instead, you want to enjoy that beautiful, liberating, downriver flow, cruising in sync with the waters, the trickling of the creek or the whitewater rafting with the rapids, changing and shifting your energy. Sometimes, it is that super high, in-tune, roaring energy of creation, of slapping waves, and other times, the constant flow of the stream and sometimes a slower drip, a continuous drip, but still in flow. And you are still allowing.

You want it to be a "Hell yeah! Feel that! Oh, yeah…" when it is right, ready and waiting! Not a "maybe," or a "perhaps," and definitely not a "later," or a "not now," or a "no"… feel the hell yeah in your bones!

Exercise: Walk and Rant

The more you stand in your power, in your creative zone of genius, the more awesome you will feel. More confident, more in alignment, more tunes up and turned on. Ask for what you want! It's time for a rant, an out loud verbal rant. Here is something I love to do myself and I want you to do it. To stand up when you ask for what you want. More embodiment, more commitment to your dreams. Showing up for all the you are and all that you desire. Think about what you want and what you want to create. The business that you desire. All the things. All the things that we have talked and written and meditated and created for you over the past several enlightening pages.

I want a rant from you! This is where you go off on a talking tangent. An excitable, inspired, beautiful rant, declaring all that you want. Your declaration of all that you are and all you want to become. The best way to do this for me is I go outside for a walk, a safe walk where I can talk out loud and record into my phone. I ask you to do this. Take that phone and the voice recording app that you have. Hit record. Walk and rant! How do you see yourself? What do you want? See it done. Think of you in the future and talk about it being done! Your business is doing good. Your work is selling. Your words are flowing. Your body feels great. You've lost the weight. You have the clients. The money is flowing. See the pieces you are creating and have created. The students you have, the classes you are teaching. See yourself on that plane, flying to your next speaking gig.

Say it out loud with intention, commitment, truth, and belief. With details and words that express it. Do you feel it? Go on for ten to twenty minutes. Fill up those minutes with *you!* You will be surprised at how this feels in your body, and once you start, you may not want it to end!

Seriously, this is an amazing exercise. The first time I did this, I thought I might be crazy or that others around me might think I was! But there's no need to imagine what others are thinking; this is your rant and yours alone. It might take doing this once or twice to get the hang of it, but once you get your mojo going, the words will start tumbling out of your mouth. Walking keeps you in motion and present in your body, so it's great to pair the two together. It really does become fun.

Twenty minutes: go.

Become a Magnet

You are becoming a magnet for what you want. Sending your desires and energy out to the universe by asking. Picturing it. Detailing it. Living it. Desire is such a strong and beautiful force. When you know what you want, you know what you don't want. Letting go of what you don't want opens you up to receive what you do want, as long as you stay focused on that. Don't even think about what you don't want anymore, put no energy and no attention on that. Continue to put your focus on how you want everything to unfold. Draw it to you. This is the Law of Attraction! (I highly suggest you start listening to podcasts by Abraham!) Being magnetic. Visualizing turns into manifestation. Remember, thoughts become words become things. That's why not just writing it down, but saying it out loud is powerful and empowering because you can feel your creative force.

Think of it this way: like attracts like. When you write your thoughts down, they become clearer, right? And saying them out loud defines them even further. It's like harnessing all your thoughts and energy and telling the universe what you want. This is rolling all the things into one big beautiful desire, Knowing, asking, allowing, receiving, appreciating, the unfolding!

The Art of Allowing

Of course, you can ask for all you want. But you want to move forward with those desires and be ready to accept them into your reality, your body, your heart, and your mind, and make them real. The next step after asking is allowing. Something for you to learn about yourself, dear one, is that you are so worth it, wo worthy of having your dreams come true. Open your heart and allow yourself this opportunity to unfold into your greatness. This is not the time to shrink back into the corner and say you are unworthy. This has nothing to do with being an introvert or an extrovert but has everything to do with you showing up in all your glory!

You are here to take up space. You are here to live full-on and experience all that life has to offer. And you are here to ask for what you want. There is an art to allowing yourself to have these things. That is creating the beauty that you are and want to be in the world, and having that happen for you. You have to want it, you have to believe it, that you can have what you are asking for, and allow yourself to have it.

With meditation, you will start to feel this allowing in your body, heart, and soul. Allow yourself to relish in this feeling, with grace. Take the time to acknowledge these changes. It's like a softening, a realization. Find peace after the past turmoil.

Now feel the appreciation that you have for all of what you are creating, and all that the universe has for you. How has your gratitude practice grown? How has your creativity grown? Your work and your ideas? Are you looking at all things differently, your work, your life? Do you feel the abundance that is waiting for you?

Here is another exercise, a different rant for you! It's good to do this one during or after your morning practice. As you've been practicing, writing, meditating, moving and shifting your energy and your body, you are asking for more abundance and success and change. What have you noticed about yourself? Take a few minutes or more and stand in front of a mirror. Look at this new you. What are you appreciating about yourself now? Tell yourself in the mirror how everything is always working out for you now. How you are feeling, all the good things! Keep the vibe positive and stay strong, show up for yourself. How much are you loving the new you? Look into your eyes. The creative, inspired, prosperous, following-through you! This is you being proud, fearless, imaginative, and even a bit quirky!

Embody all that you are wanting. Feel it in your bones, feel the tingle over your skin, the heart palpitating with excitement as all of these new desires start to unfold for you. Stand up and stretch into it. This is a good time to move the body a bit. Dance with your desires! Feel the deliciousness of your creation. Show up to it, be in it, allow it, and stand up, take up that space!

Wowza… the unfolding. I love that word. I use it a lot. I feel it in my body, as if I was an envelope and the story was unfolding out of it. Your dreams are leaping off the page. Can you feel it too? Isn't that an incredible feeling when you really allow yourself to have this thing, to create that work, and to turn on and tune in to what you are wanting to express? You take the time to shine. You are moving forward with that beautiful intention of making this happen, of living your dream. Show up in your life different than how you were. Feel the gratitude, that continuous flow of appreciation and thankfulness.

You are in your body more now, perhaps a stronger and toner body that moves with more ease too. You can feel the rhythm in your body, your own rhythm of creation, from your core and extending out all of your limbs. You just might dance a jig or stand on your head in a yoga pose.

You are more in your mind too, having connected deeper with yourself, your inner being, your source. You are not afraid to truly listen and feel your intuitive guidance, your inner light. Feel illuminated! My friend, you are showing up and that is powerful stuff.

Do you feel different, gaining in your confidence, acknowledging your desires, seeing all your possibilities and all that you want to create change?

"Today, I am ________________________.

So many things to be grateful for today: ________________________."

How will you celebrate this you that is showing up?

Another life short to share with you; to be this is about the power of being present and allowing the change. Blessings to you as we continue.

DANCE

Paulette Rees-Denis

To dance and to be danced
Water falls inside and outside
In the gathering season
Of the circle
Limbs collide
Waves swaying or pounding
The beat carries the weight
Emotions raw
I shall be released
I pray
Thankfully
Carry on legs, strong and lean
Reaching toward the heavens
Eternal search
Heart over hand over hips
Circling the dance of life
To be in it, now
Presence is required
To fully realize
The being of now

CHAPTER 10

BE A POSSIBILITARIAN

Being born, from the womb of dirt and rock
The freshiness in the air, coming alive
Oh my god, I feel the dew
The juice from the womb
And the bursting open is the rising up

~ ***Paulette Rees-Denis*** ~

WOWZA! WHAT DOES IT feel like now, to be that possibilitarian? We've gone through several ideas and steps for you to work and play with. I have shared ideas and routines to add to your daily life, to get your creativity soaring. What is resonating with you? What are you super attracted to? Do you see how you can make those changes you've been desiring, how you can fill the void deep within? To have possibilities when you thought there was none before. Now you can start that something new and step away from what is not serving you.

Does it feel easy or hard, possible or impossible? And, more importantly, how are you feeling about taking those steps?

From your daily gratitude practice and journaling, adding to your morning routines, filling in the blanks of the *I am's*, to even more physical movement and any emotional releasing of those old stories, I want to see inspirations of change on your horizon!

I'm curious, what happens to you if you don't take these steps, any or all of them? How will your job shift? What becomes of your art? Where will you be tomorrow? Where will you be a year from now? And how will you feel then, if you don't make these changes? This is important to look at, to see how committed you are… are you willing to commit forty percent, eighty percent, or 100 percent to yourself and your visions?

I bet you can feel it in your bones, the beginning of the beginning! Don't you get that tingling down your arms when you get that connection with yourself, spirit, those ah-ha moments of "Hell yeah, I can do this"!? Or what is the opposite of that? More overwhelm and self-doubt?

That's why I wrote this book for you, dear one. So you can see the light, feel the energy of all of your possibilities. I know how amazing it is to now be in this place of abundance and power and creativity. I've been in that stuck place before, too, and it's not pretty. Now it's time for you to wake up every day with joy, to have the best day of my life.

Go back to your future tripping exercise and how you were envisioning your dream job, creative project, body, and life. You laid out a pretty picture of what could be. That was a vision of a glorious you, living a great life, making money, creating art, teaching, traveling, having more free time, making more money, and being your own boss. What were you doing? How did that make you feel? Excited? Elated? Inspired? Ready to take on the world and make those changes?

If you are changing your mind or stepping back, you are stealing your dreams away from yourself. This turns into self-sabotage and that is not a nice place to be. How many times have you stopped yourself in the past? I know that story of sabotaging myself well. There have been times when I was on my way to creating something brilliant and I let something or someone else get in my way. I took a step back from what I wanted. Yes, I have been the queen of procrastination and even rebelled against myself. Hell, I even had moments like that while writing this book. It still happens to me. But not like before; never like before, because I know how to shift, how to step away and remember my desires and my purpose.

Even Elizabeth Gilbert writes about that in her *Big Magic* book, and I loved the story about how she had an idea for a new book, sat on it for a few years, and then someone else came along and wrote that same book before she could do it. I believe ideas have an energy. You get that moment of divine inspiration and often, if you don't act on it right away, it's gone.

You don't want your creative life to leave you behind. You need to act on those inspirations and divine moments of creative connection, so powerful and evocative. You can too, now, with me as your guide, whether that be here in this book, revisiting any of the exercises, or joining forces with me on the outside! I am your favorite coach, your guide to help you open those doors and take this journey to your glory of creative abundance!

What are some of the ways you can move forward? Make a list to remind you if you need that, what creates change quickly for you. And I would like to teach you something that I do almost every morning; it's my Power Walk. I combine this sometimes with my run and workout, and even a walking meditation. Those mornings that might seem a little unfocused for you, or if you are feeling stuck, this is another great way to change your state. Anytime of day is great too. Take a break, go outside so you can return to your desires! Here is a private link to my video on Vimeo. (*https://vimeo.com/228855974/f29a63d90a*)

Because, what about the ole' cliché *what if tomorrow never comes?* If not now, when? Do you think there will be a better time for you to turn your life into one of creative bliss? Do you want to wait until the kids are grown and gone, or you have more money, or you lose twenty pounds? What if you were to go through your whole life never having attempted to change and grow into that dream? Allowing yourself to stay small, quiet, unfulfilled? Would you be content, happy, satisfied? I seriously doubt it. You don't want that or you would not be reading this book!

Turn your rebel self into your sacred rebel! Honor your divine self and get out of that stuck place. You are so worth continuing on with those visions of fabulousness. Become the queen of your destiny! Shake your hips and sing that song *Worth It* by Fifth Harmony (*https://www.youtube.com/watch?v=YBHQbu5rbdQ*).

I say this over and over again. *You* have to decide. Your life is your choice, not your mother's, not your husband's, not your wife's, not your boss's. Once you make the decision, there is nothing else, there is no going back.

Get out of that self-made box. It all depends on how you set yourself up. Do you want to make up another story to hold you back or hang onto the old story or put the blame on someone else? I doubt it.

Revisit the places that have made you uncomfortable or took you out of your comfort zone. Those are the places that will move you forward with intention into your creative zone of genius. You will be stepping up and feeling so good about yourself. Find your mojo! Be that possibilitarian.

Patience and Habit-Building

Patience, grasshopper! I have to say this to myself all the time! In today's world, we are getting more and more used to getting instant gratification. Right? Some things can manifest quickly, especially when you become really good at manifesting what you desire!

You are developing those skills; the more you envision, the more you become a magnet, the more you show up, and the more the universe gives to you!

But for you here, today, be patient with yourself. You are creating new habits and new ways of working and seeing. If you rush, you may pass over those invaluable connections, with yourself and your creations. You may lose momentum by going too fast because it is easy to lose sight of your details. With patience, you are setting up a new system, physically, spiritually, and emotionally. You are potentially setting up new habits for a new life, lifestyle, and work ethic. The best way to create these new habits is to make it easy, see it as easy, and make it fun. When you start meditating, do it for a few minutes, not twenty! You'll get to fifteen or twenty in time. Make it doable and feel the flow! Keep it sustainable. You build on these new routines or rituals every day, feeling the expansion. That feels great in your body and for your whole being. And now you take the time to feel the change. Be proud of yourself and acknowledge your achievements. Tell someone, share it and let others uplift you. If you slip up, start again. No judgment. Don't beat yourself up or fall back into negative talk. Just start over and give yourself some love. Call up that good feeling.

When you get back into that funk, what'cha going to do? I'll keep reminding you to change your state! Go back to some of those ideas for changing your state, and move that body. What will feel good on your body right now?

Get outside. Do that Power Walk. Raise your energy. Shake off the procrastination, the self-doubt.

Or take a nap and reset. Take five minutes for meditation to quiet your mind and refocus. You can feel the change in your state and your momentum, daily, as you practice and shift, and practice and shift. The energy changes in your body, the mindset gets more and more committed and excited, the spirit starts to fly high.

That is your momentum kicking in. Keep your energy moving forward. Journal about the changes you are feeling. Keep up your journaling practice. I can't recommend this enough. Write about the shifts. Write about the creative ideas, the things you want to build, the ideas to build your business. Keep working with your MAP. What about the team you want to create – who do you want to work with? Who would you like to work for you? Jot down all your possibilities. Acknowledge all that you are becoming and you will feel the changes, I promise.

It's good to take the time to revisit your future self. Keep envisioning what you want and see it already done. Ask your future self what you need now to get there. You will feel more connected and closer to your vision while it begins to unfold for you. And while you are at it, keep acknowledging where you are now. As much as it is important to draw up your future ideas, being present now as you unfold is delicious. Seriously, stop and smell the roses! Feel the love right now.

Notice your choice of words. It can be easy to fall back into old habits, so be conscious every day about how you talk about yourself and your ideas and your projects. Catch yourself when you say something that can hold you back; feel it in your body. You now have the tools to change. You have the choice!

Allowing the flow, instead of fighting… this is an exquisite place to be. Feel the beauty in that place and open up to all your possibilities. My friend, you want to allow this shift, allow the current to take you. The universe has your back and so do I!

Continue to ask, what all is possible for you?

"Today, I am ______________________. Today, I am grateful for ______________________."

Let's celebrate you!

CHAPTER 11

YOU'VE GOT THE POWER

She Felt the Magic
She felt the magic burning deep in her womb,
building momentum as it sifted and shifted
through her body.
Trembling, she cruised, low riding softly,
again allowing the force to increase,
Bridging the union of her love,
With her soul.
Deep within, volcanic eruptions, waiting,
Kept simmering, shimmering,
Until the finale to overflow,
outpouring
Her desires come truly into fruition and
beauty.

~ Paulette Rees-Denis ~

You've got the power now! You are doing the work and creating your dream-come-true visions. You are creating the art you are here to make and making a difference. Can you feel it? Yes! You can feel that exquisite power and inspired visions for your creative journey deep inside you, asking you to show up and be all that you can be. With the tools and ideas I've shared with you, do you feel clearer in your heart and soul? Are you excited about what is next, and all your opportunities just waiting to open up for you?

Presence: do you feel like you are standing taller, shoulders thrown back, heart open, chest lifted, so very present in your body? Feel your feet on the earth and your head in the sky. Stay grounded, in-touch, centered, focused, tuned-in, turned-on, bursting at the seams, because this is the real you. Finally.

Your purpose is to live with your unique individual creative expression for fulfillment, wellness, with pleasure, and be the creative force behind your dreams, your art, as you move forward with intention. So, let's do this now.

You have surrendered what you were and unleashed your vibrant and wild spirit. You are ready to fly your freak flag. You have gotten in touch with your inner self, your god, your source, and you know how to ask for what you want, to make that change. From one baby step to a big leap. It may be easy and there may be some hard days, hard times. Would you trade these possibilities back in for what was?

Mapping out to your treasure chest, you follow your path and the journey unfolds with delicious work, projects, fun and rewarding to-do lists, and amazing people that you surround yourself with. You have your freedom to be, live, and create. You have learned to allow yourself to receive what the universe is offering to you because you asked for it. You are worth it.

And all this is because you are ready to be ready, to make a difference in your life and in the world. You are ready to touch someone else, to uplift them as much as we all want to continuously be uplifted, to be loved, seen, and heard.

We talked about the six basic human needs: connection and love, variety and uncertainty, certainty and comfort, significance, and then into growth and contribution. You feel all these, as we all do. You have so much to give, to offer and share, to bleed and write and compose and dance and paint. You have work to do, money to be made. You want others to feel it too.

You are moving forward with that beautiful intention of creating and rewriting this new phase of your life. Because you know you have the power and the vision and the tools to create your work, your life as you want. Your dreams are unfolding, your work is getting made, your old soulless job is gone, and how does that feel? Your time is your own, your work is calling out for you. You are a magnet and your clients are being drawn to you as you are reaching out on this new path of your career, of your entire life.

Change is happening. You are the one making that change because you have decided that now is your time. Right? If not now, when? You aren't waiting any longer because the world wants you, needs your vision, input, words, and pictures.

You've got this. I'm here for you; you know that. If we continue on with me as your coach, you mentor, your guide, I would be honored to hold that space for you to move faster and bigger into all your possibilities. I remain curious to your continued unfolding and abundance. I want to continue to support and guide and listen and watch, my reward is your continuing unfolding and expansion. To see you become a force in your creative zone, to share in your glory and illumination, your creative freedom and prosperity.

This is you, this is your life. Own it. This is you feeling connected, with juiced-up hips and belly and through every pore, every muscle, from your toes to the tip of your head, down your arms to your fingertips, just ready to move and paint and write and dance and change. Your juices are flowing; why stop? Your personal and business pleasures are ignited. You can feel the force wanting to explode out of your belly, your womb, your birthing place, your creative zone. You have raised your vibration in the world, showing up.

The world is opening up for you to show up so you can walk your talk and dance with your creative spirit. Be that beautiful, authentic person you were put on this planet to be.

That's it, that's all there is. You've become the Divine Force behind your creations and your desires. Your sacred rebel has arrived.

What else is possible?

"Today, I am grateful for the lessons, the tools, the connection, my visions, my art, my body, soul and headspace, the opportunities, and mostly the possibilities of what and all I can be and all I can give!

"Today, I am the creator of my dreams, I am in total charge of my life, I create my art with abandon and connection, allowing the flow and work and customers. I am able to enjoy the fruits of my labor and share the bounty. I have so much to give and share and create and my life is full of all that I desire. Dancing with my desires has changed my life, my work, my purpose. I feel so good and will continue on this path of self-reflection, self-care, and live my life to the fullest.

Today, I celebrate my changes, new life, new lifestyle, full of love and passion, sometimes with stepping stones and hustles and hurdles. I now know how to get through them with ease, making change, rewriting the story, and releasing the old tales of woe… I am here to celebrate all that life has to offer for me so that I can share the wealth and inspirations and make change in not only my world, but all the world!"

And today, I, Paulette, am grateful for you, my reader, for taking this journey with me and living full-on. Let's celebrate!

ACKNOWLEDGMENTS

MY HEART AND SOUL are so full of gratitude, that I have always been able to live the life I desired, the life I wrote, following that light into the wild unknown. I am deeply touched that I have been able to touch so many others with my passion and compassion, with my creative visions, and my desire to uplift others to live full on and create their life as they, too, desired. To live in a world of possibilities and beauty. And I continue to do so.

So many beautiful people have been on the journey with me, have taught me, held my hand, kicked my ass, encouraged and listened. I have had incredible support to create and continue my work in the past, and I give thanks to those that support me and also inspire me to carry on forward. The intimate tribe and global gathering of dancers, musicians, writers, teachers, clients, students, artists, creators, coaches, family, friends, who bring so much passion and love to the world, and to my world, I am continuously grateful and wowed. You all help to make our world an awe-inspiring place to live and do our work we are here to do.

I'd love to thank my editing team and tribe, along with Dr. Angela Lauria, for giving me exceptional guidance and support in writing this book, at the Author Incubator. With great encouragement and coaching from Ramses Rodriguez, and editor, Moriah Howell, who both helped shape my vision and my words, I am in gratitude. And Joy Stone, you are a godsend, thank you for always being there in this adventure.

I'm so grateful for a client who grew into an incredibly gifted entrepreneur with her paintings, teachings, and lust for life, for her painting that graces the cover of this book, Pamela Sue Johnson. Pam, you continue to inspire and awe me with your passion and heart.

And I have to thank my book cover designer, Rob Allen, and my interior book designer, Lazar Kackarovski, who worked fast and with keen eyes to help me get this in your hands.

I have always loved to dive deep, to go within, and share the treasures. That I can bring those findings, the treasure chest and the tools, here in this book to you, is a gift from me to you, so that we all can make the changes we desire to see within ourselves, and for each other.

ABOUT THE AUTHOR

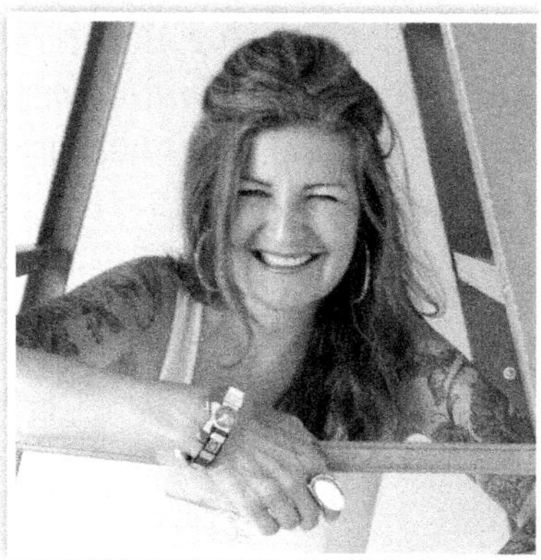

PASSION INSTIGATOR AND MOVEMENT motivator Paulette Rees-Denis is a creativity business coach, speaker, dancer, author, and a leader of feminine celebration. Paulette takes you on a journey to make changes for your creative business dreams. She gives you the tools to rewrite your story and step into your creative zone of genius. While she travels the globe, she writes from Palm Springs, California, her new home.

Paulette is the Tribal Hostess – she gathers creative women together in a variety of manners. In its third year, she interviews global small business entrepreneurs for *Heart and Hustle: Visionary Healers, Movers, and Shakers*, a bi-monthly vlog series. She has also been running Facebook Lives almost weekly for three years, with coaching, inspiration, and lively conversation as her themes. She often reads her poetry.

She is the innovator and director of the worldwide Global (Gypsy) Caravan Tribal Bellydance® and Tribal Grooves® dance styles, and the author of three books: a poetry book (*Breaking Down the Walls*), her memoir (*Tribal Vision: A Celebration of Life Through Tribal Belly Dance*), and her first book, a photographic essay (*Skin Stories: Layers of Life*).

THANK YOU

THANK YOU MY FRIEND, for showing up and doing this work. I hold you in my heart and send you heaps of support and blessings and glorious abundance as you make the transformation into your full-time creative life!

An offering for you, I'd love to gift you with my 4 week online DIY course, Dance With Desire! You can visit {*https://gypsycaravantribalbellydance.com/product/dance-desire-heart-hustle-new-online-course/*} and use this gift code upon checkout (Danceanddesiregift) so you can download today, so you can continue to build your momentum and to support you on your path. Enjoy.

Please stay in touch. I'd love to know how you are doing. I am here to offer further support and to guide you deeper into your full potential. You can contact me here and join my list here for some more fun resources too. *www.paulettereesdenis.com*,

Follow along on my Instagram, instagram.com/paulettereesdenis/, and FB pages as well... *https://www.facebook.com/tribalbellydancing*.

What all is possible for you now?

Printed in Great Britain
by Amazon

78256170R00082